Photography for

ARCHAEOLOGISTS

M. B. COOKSON

FOREWORD
BY
SIR MORTIMER WHEELER

MAX PARRISH · LONDON

MAX PARRISH AND CO LTD

55 QUEEN ANNE STREET LONDON W.I

First Published 1954

*The author's thanks are due to Lieutenant-Colonel G. W. Meates, F.S.A.,
the Society of Antiquaries of London, and the British School at Rome for
permission to reproduce photographs in their possession.*

PRINTED IN GREAT BRITAIN

BY THE CAMPFIELD PRESS ST ALBANS

PHOTOGRAPHY FOR ARCHAEOLOGISTS

General Editor

WILFRID J. MILLINGTON SYNGE

FOREWORD

I have gladly accepted the invitation to add a prefatory note to Mr Cookson's book on archaeological photography. For a quarter of a century, from Dorset to Delhi, Mr Cookson and I have striven together to induce the camera to record factually the archaeological evidence presented to it. The basic trouble is, of course, that the camera is an awful liar. Its inhuman eye and temperamental interpretation of colour-values combine to falsify the simplest of subjects, and demand a very special experience and understanding from the scientific photographer. When colour-processes become the normal medium for archaeological photography, the problem will be simplified though not eliminated. Meanwhile such information and advice as Mr Cookson has assembled during an active life were well worth putting on paper and commending to the student or practitioner.

Whether photography is an art or just a 'skill' I do not know. But I do know this: that with similar equipment and experience two men will produce astonishingly disparate results. It is clear enough that sensibility no less than sense goes to the making of the complete photographer. That is a quality which cannot be taught, even by Mr Cookson. But what the teacher can do, and in the following pages does, is to help the young photographer over a whole series of stiles, some of them formidable ones, which cross his path and obstruct achievement. The need for such a book is amply indicated by the frequency with which the standards proper to archaeological photography are still marred by avoidable defect. I wish the book all success.

MORTIMER WHEELER

London University Institute of Archaeology
April 1954

CONTENTS

ILLUSTRATIONS

To

A. E. S.

who taught me photography

R. E. M. W.

who taught me archaeology

I. W. C.

for his help with this book

I

THE VALUE AND USE OF
PHOTOGRAPHY IN ARCHAEOLOGY

Archaeology has ceased to be a simple search with a pick and a spade for a past way of life. It is nowadays supported by a series of highly skilled attendant services, such as survey, restoration in the field and in the laboratory, analysis of soils and associated remains, the keeping of systematic records and photography. With these developments in archaeology the need for and uses of photography have grown too. One cannot imagine any archaeologist today cutting even the simplest trial trench without photographing it from three or four positions, as a working record to support the plans and sectional drawings, even if not for publication.

What, then, about photography on a large site? Here it has developed into a full-time task for one person. This includes the general work of recording in the field, the copying of plans and drawings, the provision of photographs for the finds register, particularly when work is being carried out in countries where either finds or the registration book must be left behind. The completing of such a book becomes a less onerous task if aided by photography.

The main essential is, of course, good recording by photography, and this should never be stinted. Photographs of each and every section, site, wall-construction, post hole, ghost-wall and every type of construction where one living floor cuts into another, every small detail of re-building should be recorded, not only because some of these photographs will be used as illustrations for the final report, but because most of them will be referred to when writing the report and will serve to remind the writer of details that might possibly have been overlooked or not included in the site notebook.

Opinions differ on the size of the photograph which is most useful, and there is no need to take sides in the arguments for and against the miniature camera and the large plate camera. Each is good in its own particular sphere; each requires its own particular technique; but I have always used the large whole-plate camera and, expense apart, I even feel that if the finances of an excavation would allow the use of 12 in. × 10 in. plates this would well repay the additional work that would be entailed in shifting the camera from site to site.

There can be no question as to the type of photograph needed in archaeology, whether it be for definitive publication or merely for the record. It should be a clean, crisp, glossy bromide print made from a correctly exposed negative, with a wealth of shadow detail, and should convey its story at a glance, having at the same time balance and good composition.

Three main items go to the making of such a photograph: the camera and its lenses which are the tools of the trade, the sensitized material, and the light. All are of equal importance in making a success of one's efforts.

Over the camera and material we have some control; over light, if we are using daylight, very little. It is, therefore, essential to watch the play of light on a subject and to take advantage of the exact moment, because there is only one moment when a particular site looks its best from the viewpoint of the camera. Unlike the lighting of a studio photograph, in composing which the lamps can be placed at will and some pleasing effects obtained by shifting them laterally or raising or lowering them, the light on a subject in the field is only at its best for one particular moment. Fixing this ideal instant can only be done by constant watching of changing light and by noting the time at which the subject shows to the best advantage. Experience counts for a great deal, but a personal notebook with details of suitable times observed for particular sites can be extremely useful until the memory has been trained. A good plan is to fix the compass points firmly in mind as soon as a site is reached, when a rough estimate of the correct moment can always be made from a known point of the sun's position, due south at noon.

Whilst a high degree of technical skill and knowledge of camera craft is essential, that alone is not enough. It must be coupled with realization that the task of the archaeological photographer is scientific recording, which demands the utmost integrity. Pencil, knife or brush must never touch the negative once it has been made. Retouching of negatives is acceptable in commercial and portrait photography, but in archaeology the accentuation of features must be done either on the site or section itself, with trowel, penknife, brush and water, or by use of light filters with the camera lens. Both methods will be discussed in later chapters.

Following good craftsmanship, experience and scientific integrity comes, lastly, Cleanliness of the subject with a capital C. Although it is mentioned last, I sometimes think it should come first, for no matter how correct the exposure and the development of the negative, no matter how carefully a print is made, a wall with mud still clinging to it, a floor poorly brushed, a pavement insufficiently washed, the badly-trimmed grass edge of a cut can completely ruin the finest of photographs from an archaeological standpoint. From experience, I know how heart-breaking it can be to scrape a stone floor hour after hour, or to wash the metalling of a Roman road pebble by pebble until I hoped that every stone would come loose and there would be an end to any photograph – but I know also the pleasure the ultimate result has brought when the photograph of the finished work is seen. Some of these words on cleanliness will appear again; they cannot be over-emphasized. ALWAYS KEEP THE SITE CLEAN! Cleaned stone and chalk glisten in the light, their shapes show sharp and clean when the earth on which they lie is undercut and they are well brushed.

A sharp right-angle where the last archaeological layer meets 'natural', balks swept at the end of a day's work, will repay the trouble taken a hundredfold. If the excavation lasts several weeks, regular cutting of the grass on the balks will help, when, at the last, the photographs of the site are to be taken. If not, the grass may have grown out of hand, needing the attention more of a scythe than a simple pair of gardening shears. All these things, if done in good time, will save hours when photographs have to be taken and the closing time of the excavation draws near.

2

THE LARGE FIELD CAMERA,
ITS LENSES, FILTERS AND TRIPODS

This is a department in which any shortcomings will make themselves felt insistently. Therefore I do recommend a slow, studied care when purchasing equipment. The best way to approach this subject is to put on paper every item that is likely to be required and to circulate such a list to first-class dealers only. Having then obtained estimates and viewed equipment, the simplest method is to allow one dealer to supply all the items. Piecemeal collection of lenses and filters from various dealers does not pay. Find one dealer to help you and you have his complete interest, not only in your work in general and in making the immediate sale, but in any further servicing which may be required. This applies whether the intention is to use the miniature or the large field camera.

Let it be assumed that an expedition is starting from scratch as regards photography. Whilst there is to be no cheese-paring, each purchase must be keen and of good quality. The equipment will need an active life of perhaps five seasons, with only reconditioning and no renewals. Assuming that we are to work with the larger field camera our needs would be as follows:

1 A field camera of strong construction.

2 At least six dark slides, each to hold two plates.

3   Three lenses: (*a*) a lens of long focal length, (*b*) a lens of medium focal length, (*c*) a short-focus or wide-angle lens.

The approximate focal lengths of these lenses correspond to the diagonal measurement of the plate in use for the long focus, the measure of the long side of the plate for medium focus and the measure of the short side of the plate for the short focus or wide angle.

4   Ring adapters for fitting these lenses into the one lens panel.

5   A set of filters, possibly consisting of a red, a green and a deep yellow. The reason for and use of these filters will be dealt with in full in later chapters.

6   A very stout tripod, much heavier than the size of the camera actually demands. It should be adjustable as to height from 2 ft. 6 in. from the ground-level to 6 ft. and the head on which the camera is screwed should be able to tip over to 90° and enable the camera to be used vertically. (Always take a spare camera screw in the case.)

7   An essential is a 6-in. bubble level. The small circular type of level attached to cameras is seldom trustworthy and when photographing small hills, mounds and sections, it is most essential to obtain a true horizon.

8   Lens hoods, shutters and other small oddments. I would hesitate to make too many suggestions about these, for many photographers have their own pet ideas and when assembling such an outfit these essential oddments are generally collected by the way.

9   An extremely strong case to carry the camera and all the accessories. This will have to be made, unless a really

1. *PREPARATION OF A SITE for the photographer; a fine example.
Note that all levels consist mainly of sand – these quickly dry into dust and make
right-angle cuts almost impossible. (F.32. 5 secs. First light. No filter.)*

2. *PROBLEMS OF CONTRAST.* Above: *Red-brown oven remains brought up by green filter against counterlit yellow wet clay. (F.32. 6 mins. Tricolour green filter. Diffused light.)* Below: *Post-holes in yellow clay gravel. This subject was dry, and thus easily cleaned. (F.32. 6 mins. Tricolour green filter. Weak, flat, diffused light.)*

strong second-hand case suitable for the task can be found. They do exist, but need some search.

When purchasing lenses, it must be remembered that the use of a very wide-aperture or 'fast' lens is seldom necessary in field archaeology, in which exposures are normally made from the stand. It is better, therefore, to purchase first-quality Anastigmat lenses which will work at apertures of, say, F.6·3 or F.8. These will be found quite useful, because larger-aperture lenses of any considerable focal length, working at F.3·5 or F.4·5 are extremely large and weighty and give a deal of resistance to wind. A really large focusing cloth should be provided, which can be used to protect the camera if sudden rain occurs. Spare lens caps should also be carried, and several pieces of ground glass as replacements, should the focussing-screen be broken.

If working in out-of-the-way places it is difficult, if not impossible, to obtain really fine-grained ground glass. Even after finding it, having it cut to fit into the camera-back is nerve-racking, when you see the only available piece of glass being cut by an inexpert hand and with a blunted wheel-cutter!

Mention has been made of the lens working at F.8 and F.6·3. This 'F' system is a scale designed to express the 'speed' of light transmission of the lens. The smaller the 'F' number the larger the aperture and the more light reaches the plate or film.

When using the smallest F. number provided, i.e. F.8 or F.6·3, the camera is said to be working at 'full aperture'. Round the lens are inscribed other markings representing round fractions of the large or full aperture, such as F.11 (half F.8), F.16 (half F.11), F.22 (half F.16), and these are brought into use when greater definition is required. For example, when copying a flat drawing or picture it should only be necessary to use, say, F.16, because if the drawing has been centred correctly and the camera set parallel with the drawing, it is simply recording one plane and there is no depth of focus required. In the case of a pot, or a medium view, the depth from the nearest portion of the subject facing the lens to the more distant parts is considerable, and increases with the size of the image obtained on the ground-glass screen. Therefore, to get the front and back simultaneously in focus it becomes necessary to 'stop down' or decrease the aperture to, say, F.32 or F.45. In this stopping down the amount of light reaching the sensitive plate is being reduced and exposure must therefore be increased. A rough adjustment for the 'stopping down' is to *double* the exposure at each smaller aperture used, i.e. if 10 seconds is given at F.8 then 20 seconds must be given at F.11 and so on.

For some sites where there are many trees and especially when there is much wind, or there are moving cattle in the picture, a shutter is extremely useful. A shutter that will fit two of the lenses in the equipment will be a boon. It need only work at 1/25 and 1/50 of a second.

Whilst I have suggested three lenses of varying focal length to be sufficient for the average site, the addition of a telephoto lens may prove useful even if it is only used two or three times in a season. One of the older types, say the Dallon which gives a very fair magnification with a small extension of camera, is entirely suitable if well 'stopped down'. This, too, can be made to fit into the existing lens panel by means of adaptor rings. One large master-ring screwed into the panel, with all the lenses fitting to it by varying sizes of rings, will be found most efficient, and far smoother working will be obtained this way than by having a panel for each lens.

Six double dark slides were specified as a minimum earlier in this chapter. This may seem unnecessarily many but will undoubtedly save time during a full day when it is not easy to return to Headquarters darkroom and reload. Of course, there is such a thing as a 'changing bag', but it is likely to be most cumbersome with the larger type of plate or film ($6\frac{1}{2} \times 8\frac{1}{2}$ or 8×10). I carry 10 double dark slides and always start my day fully loaded. All dark slides should be numbered in bold figures and a system must be evolved for returning exposed plates to the case in such a way that there can be no possibility of double exposures. In my early days as a commercial photographer I was, at one time, one of five cameramen, out early and back late, doing a multiplicity of jobs. We had a system whereby the indoor staff could open up any camera that came in and take out the exposed plates, leaving the unexposed, with never a mistake. That system I use today. With the camera case facing me and opening from me, I keep all my slides on the right-hand side of the case, then if I use No. 1, it goes back to the front where it came from, only with the *draw slide down*. If then I use No. 2, I shall have completed a slide and it goes to the *back* of the dark slides, *draw slides down*, and so on, until I have used all my slides. If I only use one or two complete slides, then those *draw slide down* are exposed. This is only one idea; others may evolve some other system, but having worked out a system, stick to it.

The tripod or stand, I have said, should be heavier than the camera requires; this strength is needed for wind resistance and ability to stand up to the very harsh treatment equipment receives in the field. Moreover, a heavy stand can give added confidence if the camera position is high up or in an awkward place. The tipping or tilting head is convenient for two reasons: (i) the adjustment of the picture is quick and (ii) it is often necessary to photograph vertically on finds *in situ* and skeletal remains, or, on occasion, to tip upwards.

I doubt if there is any other type of specialist camera work which calls for such a variety of movements with the camera or the stand as archaeology. Other specialist cameramen go to work knowing exactly what they are going to do – the specialist on interiors photographs interiors only, the machinery photographer has his camera adapted to suit his class of work, so does the portraitist and the man specializing in oil paintings – but the equipment of an archaeological photographer has to do every type of task from a simple view to the photography of a minute object at twice its actual size, *in situ*, and he must have the gear in his case and be able to take advantage of its adaptability.

Since the keynote of adaptability is so prominent it follows that the light filters should also be adaptable. This may prove a little difficult because lenses of varying focal length are naturally of varying diameters, and if equipment is to be kept as light as possible a set of filters for each lens, if there are only three, means nine filters – quite a costly matter. Therefore, some arrangement for making the filters adaptable to at least two of the lenses should be made. I am inclined to favour the spring-clip variety and to use them on the *back* of the lens. This means removing the ground-glass screen for each change of filter, but the operation will pay in the long run for two reasons: firstly, the same lens cap as before can be used – which is impossible if there is a filter on the front of the lens – and secondly, if, after making an exposure the camera is hoisted away and the filter drops off, it drops on to the bellows and can be retrieved unbroken. So I recommend the clip-type, or possibly the spring-type fitting on each of the three filters. Three filters are specified because I have found that three is ample – a red, or deep orange, a green and a K3 (a deep yellow). Their uses are explained in a later chapter.

3

THE HAND-OR-STAND CAMERA
AND THE MINIATURE CAMERA

The foregoing chapter dealt with the larger type of camera that I favour, but the miniature and the hand-or-stand camera have many advocates and cannot be forgotten, if only on the score of economy. Since we are thinking in terms of decreasing size let us take the 'hand-or-stand' camera first.

Hand-or-stand cameras are generally made to take a plate or film 9×12 cm. or quarter-plate, or $3\frac{1}{4} \times 4\frac{1}{4}$ in., the last a very useful size and format suitable for archaeology. The use of this type of camera does strike a middle note between the whole-plate at one end of the scale and the miniature at the other. This type is not in much use today, fashion having trended towards the smaller camera, although many serious amateur workers still use it. Being out of fashion, such cameras are reasonable in price and can be bought for something between fifteen and twenty guineas. They are highly suitable for a small dig, always provided that enlarging can be done easily by the operator: if the negatives have to be sent out to be enlarged costs will, of course, rise. The movements required for most types of work are incorporated in this type of camera – the rising and falling lens panel, the swinging back and the double or triple extension enabling the operator to take photographs at life-size. Used on a strong, heavy stand, most jobs can be done with it. It can also be used as a hand camera, since it is fitted with a sector shutter. For any standard model a lens panel can be made to take a wide-angle lens, and since focussing is carried out on the usual ground-glass screen it simply becomes the small brother of the whole plate camera, provided always that its capacity is enhanced by a sufficient number of dark slides. For a long series of small jobs – a one-man excavation shall we say, or a number of 'tip and run' surveys when weight counts – this type of equipment is exactly what is required.

Filters and lens hood may be obtained to fit and, with the whole in a small case, you have an extremely useful piece of equipment. Though prices, as we have seen, are very favourable, always buy from a reputable dealer, not from second-hand furniture stores or pawnshops. Cameras of any kind bought like this may need new bellows, shutter adjustments or even major overhaul, so that the 'bargain' becomes costly in renovation before it is ever taken into the field.

As for the miniatures, their devotees often show large prints and ask if it 'isn't as good as the whole-plate'. One must admit that on occasion the answer is 'yes'. In the case of a worker who has specialized in miniature work for years, again 'yes'. There is no question that the better-class miniature camera does excellent work in skilled hands, but it does require a specialized technique both in its operation and in the processing of the film.

Even the miniature camera still needs a battery of lenses – a long-focus, say 13·5 cm., a medium of 5 cm. and a wide-angle lens. A heavy tripod is still indispensable. Further, 'takes' must be checked either immediately after exposing or at the end of a day. There may be 12 or 36 shots on each reel and cutting is tedious and unavoidably wasteful. Although the film is cheap, the wastage in film, processing materials and time has to be considered. Another disadvantage is the magnified effect of poor processing or processing under difficulties. Pinholes, scratches and other blemishes do inevitably occur however carefully the operations are carried out. Very little can be done for a tiny film marked with scratches or pinholes when it has to be enlarged to eight diameters.

I have seen several seasons' work with the 35mm. so well executed that it was a revelation, a thing to enjoy. In that particular instance the magnifying results made me wonder why I still carried all that heavy gear, but that was only a single occasion. I have often been tempted to change to a miniature camera and once did actually make some furtive experiments, but I was soon back again to my old love, in the middle of the season. I decided to remain old-fashioned and reserve my 35mm. for colour shots.

In the larger format of $2\frac{1}{4} \times 2\frac{1}{4}$ in. there are cameras of the Reflex type with the Proxar lenses for close detail. Here again there are still 12 exposures on a roll with all the drawbacks already listed for the 35mm. range. Excellent work is being done with these cameras, the results of which are to be seen in our popular magazines, but I still do not think that they are downright suitable for standard field photography in archaeology. They are light to carry and if one is compelled to dig and photograph alone then a Reflex provides a working compromise, but mastery of the camera and its operation, mastery in processing the smaller materials, is essential.

The types of equipment I have mentioned have, in the main, called for the expenditure of considerable sums of money, but there are excavations that have to be carried out on less than the proverbial shoe-string. If, for example, photographs are needed of church or masonry details and funds are not available for a high-class instrument, I see no reason why an ordinary folding camera should not serve, with due precautions. Whilst with a good miniature of the Reflex type focussing and composition of the picture are seen to be correct, as is also the case with the range-finder type of miniature, the folding camera can be used by adjusting the distance of the subject from the lens to one of the distances engraved round the lens panel. In such cases I recommend the use of a tape-measure to ensure accuracy, particularly with the smaller distances. Some people make a habit of guessing the distance. This guess is frequently wrong.

A simple and infallible procedure is to get the area required into the view-finder, check the foreground distance with the tape-measure and then stop down to F.16 or F.22. At these small apertures the exposure given by the light meter must be multiplied by the appropriate factors, i.e. if the meter gives 1/10 second at F.8, then the exposure will be 1/5 second at F.11, and 2/5 second at F.16. No shutter is designed to give 2/5 second so the nearest larger exposure indicated should be used, which is probably half a second. There is nothing, short of a gale, to prevent the use of F.32 or F.45 to obtain maximum depth of focus, providing the camera is on a stand. Never attempt hand-held exposures of longer than 1/25 second, and remember that anything up to 1/100 is improved by the use of a stand. Double the exposure is required for each successive smaller stop. Attempts to photograph small objects or to approach closer than three feet with the folding camera (the non-viewing variety) must be discouraged. The view-finder is not adjusted for parallax (lateral distance from the optical axis of the lens) at these short distances, and the image seen in the view-finder will not be the same as that given by the resulting negative. This is called 'cut off' and is avoidable. Constant practice with a camera of this sort will tell how much 'play' actually exists, or the distance between the axis of the camera lens and that of the view-finder can be measured and due allowance made on a scale in the field of view when composing the picture.

These hints are given in passing in the hope that they may be of use in the case of a student preparing illustrations for a thesis or a beginner just making a start, where money for anything more expensive is not available.

4

MATERIALS

The term 'materials' includes plates, cut or sheet film, roll films and miniature negative stock. Today, materials are practically perfect – free from coating faults, with an almost uncanny constancy of speed and sensitivity in every batch manufactured over a period of years. The feeling for, and knowledge of, the possibilities of the material can only come with constant handling. Just as a carpenter or joiner knows the quality and the possibilities of the wood with which he works, so the photographer should be familiar with his materials.

In photography both the expert and the amateur often swear by such-and-such a make of film and aver that no other can ever come up to the high standard of work given by the particular brand or type of material they use. This, of course, means that the person concerned has full experience of that type of material, knowing that it will serve under the conditions in which he uses it, and the method he adopts to process it. In fact all photographic materials today are excellent. The manufacturers set out to make them perfect and in my opinion very nearly succeed.

Consider for a moment a modern sensitized material. It consists of a sheet of celluloid, glass or paper of accurate thickness coated with an emulsion. One type of emulsion will give a rendering in monochrome of colour, light and shadow all in their correct tonal proportions. Another emulsion may be of such contrast that it can faithfully reproduce a line engraving in black and white without half-tones. One is obliged to marvel – I do still when I open a new packet of film, with its specially prepared interleaving papers, foil wrapping and cardboard box – and not least at the price. Every photographer can have full confidence, knowing of the care, skill and scientific pride that go to the making of the material. I always try, if time permits, to take my students to the factories in order that they may see the material produced and thereby learn a proper respect for it.

Success in photography – and by that I mean the regular production of good negatives and prints under varying conditions – will be due in no small measure to the excellence of modern photographic materials, but to this must be added the familiarity of the operator with the quality and speed of the material and its response to the type of developer chosen for the processing.

There are three main types of material which will be of service to us in archaeological photography:

1	PROCESS MATERIAL (having blue sensitivity)	Suitable only for the reproduction of black-and-white diagrams, tracings on linen.
2	ORTHOCHROMATIC (yellow-green sensitivity)	For making copies of subjects having tone values; some types of pottery, glass, brick, stone walls, sandstone.
3	PANCHROMATIC (sensitive to all colours including red)	Sky rendering, adaptability with contrast filters, sections, and general work upon most sites.

On most sites there often arises the necessity for photo-graphing plans and drawings, and also drawings for the Finds Register. These are mostly carried out in indian ink on white or blue-squared paper and, since we wish to reproduce the contrast given by the dead-black ink and the white paper, we use process emulsion. This, of course, can be done only where there is a settled H.Q. and a fitted darkroom, but as the necessity sometimes arises in the field, and during long periods on a site abroad, it is as well if the site photographer has with him a small amount of process material in case the need should arise.

It sometimes happens, however, that copies from books, watercolours, or slightly coloured plans are needed, requiring colour correction only to a small degree. Then the ortho-chromatic or yellow-green emulsion is used. For general work, the panchromatic or red-sensitive emulsion will be found to be best because of its sensitivity to all colours. With correct exposure this gives a tone-rendering in monochrome of all colours with a close approximation to what the eye sees.

Since panchromatic material has these properties, it can be used with various light-filters and by this means a variety of contrasts can be obtained. For most purposes, then, the pan-chromatic material is best suited to archaeological needs mainly because of its adaptability and latitude. The grade adopted for general use on a site is *not* suitable for line or dia-gram reproduction and it is therefore essential to carry a little of the process material if there is the slightest possibility of black-and-white copying work, particularly if you are working overseas.

Yellow-green or orthochromatic material, excellent though it is, will not render reds in correct tone and therefore has limitations when it is a question of demonstrating archaeological stratification. If, on the other hand, the subject anticipated is nothing but white buildings against a sandy-coloured earth, then the 'ortho' will serve admirably, because it can be used with a yellow or light-green filter to obtain varying contrasts. However, unless a definite type of subject without red detail of any kind is to be photographed, it is better to be provided with red-sensitive material and gain contrasts by the use of filters.

In the studio with every facility to hand it is possible to have in stock a choice of three or four types of panchromatic material, orthochromatic material, and three or four kinds of process or photo-mechanical emulsions. There we have the choice of artifical light or daylight, and varying types of developer to suit each emulsion. This is obviously impossible in the field. Darkroom conditions are more difficult, storage sometimes a problem. Most of the time available will be spent on the site recording and, providing supplies are sufficient for the general run of work, the smaller the variety of stock the less the work will be.

One further point: if glass plates are chosen as against a sheet or cut film, they must be of the *backed* variety, in order to cut down halation. Halation is the spread of density of exceptional highlights on to other portions of the negative, and this 'spread' tends to obliterate adjacent detail. It is particularly noticeable when photographing in wooded areas where bright patches of sky shine through gaps in foliage, or where ramparts and mounds are silhouetted against the sky, or where windows feature in interior photographs.

Halation cannot be altogether eliminated; it can, however, be minimized to a great extent by the use of 'backed' plates or, using an old term now seldom used, by 'anti-halation' films. All brands of film are nowadays treated to minimize halation, but the necessity for backing does apply to glass plates. As its name implies, it is a material coated on the back, or glass, side of the plate and washes off during development. In the case of film, it is a soluble dye. Whether applied to plates or film it does not affect the life of the developer.

I would not give special recommendation to any particular make of film or plate . . . all are good. I have my own particular fancy, which I have used since 1945 – an improvement on the brand I was using up to 1939 – but I have heard others condemn it and therefore it would seem to be a matter of personal choice.

A good plan, when searching for a suitable material, is to make tests, under given standard conditions of light, exposure and development, of several brands; then, having selected one, to use it under varying conditions – simulated conditions if the real thing is not possible – always keeping good notes to check results. Having made a choice, stick to it; changing from one material to another without first confirming correct exposure, time of development, and the temperature of the developer will not eliminate failures. Technique is more likely to be at fault than the material. Gaining knowledge of the material's capabilities is a matter of experience, but constant use and the conscientious keeping of a log-book will take you a long way towards success.

The keeping of this log-book need not be a complicated matter – something in the manner of the table opposite about five or six columns – but it should be used each time an exposure is made; then after development has taken place a check can be made as to the suitability of the negative, its density, and its rendering of highlights and shadow details. Its general quality can be judged against the notes, and if the negative appears over-exposed or under-exposed, then a fresh exposure might be made and either stop or shutter speed adjusted to produce a negative of better quality –

provided, of course, that full consideration is given to the notes made in the log-book.

COOME 1953

SITE	TIME	LIGHT REQD	EXPOSURE DETAILS	REMARKS
FROM 'A' LOOKING TOWARDS CHURCH	11.30 a.m.	BRIGHT SUN		
'B' TRENCH III LOOKING E.	3.00 p.m.	NO SUN		
'A' CAUSEWAY & BASTION LOOKING E.	11.30 a.m.	STRONG SUN	10" LENS F22 2 SECS NO FILTER	PASSED OK NEG NO 135

This system of recording such data as light, stop, exposure etc. is a good thing, particularly with anyone starting photography. I recommend it to my students, and I have found that the student who adopts such a system rarely if ever comes to consult me once a good start has been made on these lines. In practice I also find that these students are the people who produce the most intelligent work with a minimum of waste.

When in the field I keep a log myself, and for the record write the details on my negative and negative bag.

Even in the studio where conditions of light have little variation, I always keep a record of unusual tasks, noting position and strength of lights, material, background details – every item that is likely to prove of use should a similar task appear again. In fact, it has become an unwritten law that the unusual job is recorded, and it has proved its worth time and time again.

Earlier in this book (p. 20) mention was made of filters. These form an important part of the equipment. There are about a hundred types of filter made for every possible class of photography, but for archaeological purposes the selection can be reduced to three: a 'tricolour' red, a 'tricolour' green and a deep yellow. As with the material, simplify whenever possible; avoid having to worry about numerous filters. These three will answer any situation that may occur on any site.

The filters are sheets of gelatine dyed to a standard colour and cemented between pieces of specially prepared glass, which are then mounted in circular holders with a bayonet or spring-clip fastening to attach them to the lens. If, as previously suggested, there are three, four or five lenses among the equipment, the chances are that a double set of filters will be necessary, since the varying focal lengths of the lenses give them varying diameters.

A filter will allow some colours to pass and reach the emulsion whilst others will be absorbed. For example, a red filter transmits red whilst stopping blues and greens; a deep yellow will cut out the blue and yet allow most of the other colours in the spectrum to pass. As the capabilities of the material will by now have become familiar, it is known that it will render certain colours in such a tone, with the aid of a

Cleaning poor

Grass not cut

Dump near edge

Edges not sharp

3. *CLEANLINESS, CLEANLINESS, CLEANLINESS . . .*

4. MASONRY. Above: *Well cleaned, correctly lit.* Below: *Patchy lighting, poor preparation. Tiling course on left is partly 'lost.'*

particular light filter. Thus we have here yet more control of the rendering of soil-colours in the stratification of archaeological layers. By allowing the light from the subject to pass through a filter, tone-contrasts can be obtained between parts of the subject of the same tonal value but of different colour.

The filter can be used by placing it either in front of the lens or behind it and focussing should be done with the filter in position. Whether in front or behind does not matter so long as the filter fits securely. If asked for a practical preference I would unhesitatingly recommend the back position, because sometimes there may be a shutter on the front of the lens and, even if the exposure is made by the removal of the lens cap, the presence of the filter on the front will necessitate the use of a larger cap and this is yet another small item to be provided. Again, if the filter is on the back of the lens and is knocked off by an accidental jar, it falls on to the bellows without risk of being broken.

One main consideration is the increase of exposure necessary when any of these filters is in use. Each filter is of a standard density. A practical allowance is to give the tricolour red four times the exposure, the tricolour green six times the exposure and the deep yellow twice the exposure. These are known as the filter factors, for increasing the exposure to compensate for the light absorbed by the filter chosen. There are slight variations in the response of different materials to the light passed by the standard colour-filters. These are always given on a slip of paper enclosed with the film, so that slightly different factors may have to be used for the same filter with the different materials. Materials do vary by a very little from batch to batch of film or plates, but the round factors given above will be found perfectly satisfactory in most cases.

c

If there has not been time to acquire sufficient experience to say at once which filter is to be used, the section may be viewed through the filter held in the hand, when its effect on the tonal values will be apparent. Though sections and recording of stratification are extremely important, there are many other ways in which the filters can be used. For instance the use of a red or yellow filter will darken the blue of a sky and show up clouds in white contrast. A landscape, however lovely, loses its beauty entirely in a photograph which reproduces it with a plain white sky, while the clouds make a picture out of it. Similarly the pleasing white columns of buildings against a dark sky can be very beautiful, indeed dramatic, when the filter brings them up. Without it their luminosity under the sun is lost in the general flood of light. Whilst the main job is to record accurately, if the opportunity presents itself the record should be given pictorial value as well. These suggestions are made on the understanding that the photographs are taken at the normal exposure, but slight under-exposure and prolonged development will build up an even greater contrast with clouds, and white buildings against a blue sky.

Sometimes in landscapes a haze can be seen to obscure the horizon. If it is desired to eliminate this the red or yellow filter can be used with good effect. Many a time on a winter's afternoon I have had to photograph a view from a site and if the distance has been misty I have exposed through a red filter – thus obtaining my distant details. On such occasions, however, the exposure must be 'cut'. If there is the least wind the long grass in the foreground, or the trees, may move.

A word on the purchase of filters. They are, as I have said, pieces of gelatine dyed to standard and cemented between two sheets of specially prepared glass. Two grades of glass exist, known as A glass and B glass. For archaeological purposes the B glass will serve. The A glass is the more expensive and is generally used in a studio for colour reproduction work. Great care should be exercised when purchasing filters. It would be as well to take the camera to the dealer's, fit the lenses and then try on the filter whilst the camera is set up. This is essential when filters are to fit on the back of the lens, since the adaptor rings holding the lens may interfere with precise fitting. Being assured that they do fit snugly, see to it that each filter has its own case, marked on the outside with its colour to save time in handling

In the field, I am a firm believer in having every filter in a complete set in its own mounts. Some workers keep one mount and separate filters. Some even go to the length of inserting a piece of the filter gelatine between the lens components. The latter is a bad practice in the field, even in good weather, and ill-treatment of a lens, which is not designed to have its back and front elements constantly being separated. Besides, it is a waste of time. Filters, like lenses, are necessary and not inexpensive items of equipment. Since even normal careful work in the field is hard on equipment, each filter and each lens should have its own strong case. Every effort should be made to return filters to their cases immediately after exposing. Cleaning of filters should be done only with a piece of old, well-washed silk or the tissues now on sale for cleaning spectacles.

6

LIGHT

Sharp observation of light is essential if an archaeological photograph is to have life. There can be no 'this will do' attitude towards the lighting of a worthwhile subject. It can be safely said that there is only one quality of light which renders a subject at its best and, because work on a site is practically always in daylight, the particular section or area of work has to be constantly watched in order to get the utmost from it. The subject should be observed at short intervals under varying conditions of light, the time of each visit noted, and short memoranda of special points entered in the notebook, until it is seen beyond doubt which lighting conditions are most likely to emphasize successfully the points to be illustrated.

There are times when strong sunlight would completely spoil a photograph, other occasions when a diffused light would kill the subject by giving it a flat, lifeless appearance. A trench-section of which half is in deep shadow is impossible to photograph successfully. It is essential to see the bottom of a trench, and strong sunlight, giving heavy shadows in contrast, obliterates all detail and makes it look like a neatly cut hole in the ground. In this case, obviously, a moment of diffused light should be chosen, when the sun is obscured by cloud, or even an altogether overcast day when some 'pick-up' contrast can be made in the printing.

Again, very oblique lighting by strong sunlight on the face of a stratified section will only intensify the inequalities of its surface, every projection of earth casting a deep shadow, and giving a pock-marked effect completely obscuring the stratification. Such a section demands a soft, even and not intense light, preferably at a rather acute angle, avoiding any heavy shadows. This particular quality of light would probably be useless for brick or stone walls, which would require a quite different treatment.

Masonry with well-defined courses might answer to a side light falling at an angle of 45°, whilst a mud-brick wall, the bricks of which rarely stand out well, needs a strong and very oblique light from above if the character of its construction is to be revealed. Slight brick masonry or rubble foundations will need a low oblique light to show the plan of the building, unless, of course, they are of colour or tone contrasting with the soil on which they are laid. Such contrasts will be improved by good cleaning, when the camera position can afford to be higher, looking down on the foundations in the manner of an air-photograph.

Thus, subjects which have little relief require strong oblique lighting, which means, in this country, an early-morning or late-evening sun. Close-ups of meeting walls at right angles sometimes present difficulty, for it is a good principle to have one face well lit and the abutting face in some slight degree of shadow in order to obtain a sense of depth in the picture.

So far, we have been considering orthodox lighting either from the right or left of the camera, high or low as the subject demands. There is another sort of lighting of which many photographers are shy. This is the counter-light from in front of the camera. It is not really a bogey, as some people seem to think. Some amazingly good effects can be obtained, not necessarily pictorial only, but good technical effects. Working against the light involves the use of a good lens hood. Failing that, the lens may be shielded with a sheet of cardboard or wood (I have used a hand shovel before now). For success, the extent of the field of view of the lens must be known; for example, with a lens of great focal length the field of view is narrow, so that the shield can be held well down over it. Great care must be taken with the wide-angle lens, or the shield may be in the field and cut off part of the subject. There is a limit to the liberties to be taken with counter-light. To aim the lens straight into the sun is, of course, disastrous and it is impossible to make a general rule as to the limits. Experience alone will tell how close one can afford to go with the particular lens area, but it is an extremely useful 'dodge' and, properly carried out with a correctly shielded lens, can give the most pleasing results.

The lighting of earthworks, banks, ditches and causeways must always be carefully watched if these structures are to have meaning in the picture. Seldom is an even light any use. The field of view is always somewhat flattened even by the long-focus lens, and if a wide-angle lens is employed then the field tends to appear flatter than ever. Thus it is essential to have really strong light which will flood the causeways. One line of rampart may be in full light, so the one nearest the camera should be in heavy shadow; in other words, accentuate the relief by the use of suitable lighting, trying to produce the effect of depth and distance. There is, generally speaking, only one time of day when this is possible, when one mound stands well out from the other in strong relief; it may be in the early morning, at midday, or at the setting of the sun. The desired moment can only be found by forethought, planning and careful watching, and caught by being ready to expose at the critical instant.

General work on a site may include as subjects – according to the type of site – mosaic pavements, skeletal remains and finds *in situ*. These will require just as much care in the choice of light as the earthwork or general views of the site. A later chapter will be devoted to the choice of the best lighting for each such subject.

Although artificial light does not enter a great deal into archaeological photography (except for cave excavations) a few words about it may not come amiss while the subject of light is to the fore. Some time ago I was amazed to be told by an archaeologist that he had recently photographed a tomb by means of mirrors, catching the daylight in one mirror and passing the light along to the subject by reflecting it with other mirrors. The resulting negatives were of very uneven quality, and since I had the task of conjuring prints out of them (they were all under-exposed!) I felt that ingenuity had been carried a little too far. If proper recording of subterranean sites is to be attempted at all, the purchase of some form of artificial lighting would be a good investment. After all, the considerable expenditure on lenses and cameras surely justifies the little more necessary to ensure efficient lighting giving a standard intensity of light and exposure at a given lens aperture. The following types of equipment are available:

1 Portable electric flashlight with its own battery giving a guaranteed 10,000 flashes before renewal is necessary.

2 Flash-bulbs, small and large.

3 Flash-powder, which is once more on the market.

4 Magnesium ribbon.

5 Electric filament lamps working from a car battery.

6   Lighting powered by a small dynamo on the back of a truck.

7   A high-power dry-battery lamp.

All of these, correctly used, will give even lighting, for which a standard exposure can be calculated. They are extremely easy to use with the possible exception of flash-powder, which should never be set off in a small enclosed space. Magnesium ribbon can be ignited in various positions and quite effective lighting can be obtained with it at small cost. Flash-bulbs are, of course, preferable for clean work and if several pictures are to be made in a short time the electric flash or flash-bulbs are indispensable. Flash-powder and magnesium ribbon both make a certain amount of white smoke and further exposures cannot be made without loss of subject detail until this has dissipated. The automatic flash or flash-bulbs give a definite light and one flash is normally enough if only small areas are to be covered by the picture. With larger areas, two, three or even four flashes may be necessary, and there is no danger from this equipment in confined spaces or where the ceilings are low.

The amount of flash-powder or the proper length of magnesium ribbon is, of course, measured. If the amounts are kept constant and are used at a given stop, they will give a standard quality of negative. Longer exposures necessitate either a larger amount of flash-powder or ribbon or a larger aperture of the lens. Flash-powder is either ignited by means of a proper percussion-cap on a tray, or it can be spread evenly over a piece of wood and lit by a match. In the latter case a fuse is first made with a little piece of cotton-wool on which some flash-powder has been sprinkled, laid in contact with the full charge. Magnesium ribbon is sold in a convenient holder and a given length is pulled out and ignited.

With both these methods, the utmost care must be taken or accidents may result.

To return once again to the use of daylight: general rules cannot be made. Only by constantly watching can one see what looks best. A simple way to become familiar with problems of light is to look at everything as though it were to be photographed. Even in cities there are subjects for exercise, in the play of light on buildings and in the parks, on trees, open spaces and flower beds. To look at anything and everything as one goes along, considering whether or not it makes a suitable subject for a picture, soon gives one an appreciation of light, and an idea of how to meet, photographically, the varied problems it presents.

7

THE SCALE

All archaeological photographs must have a scale. This is indispensable – a photograph without a scale is useless because no idea can be formed of the size of the subject.

Properly to understand a photograph of any subject, the mind has first to form some idea of the size of the objects in the picture. A comparison with something of known dimensions is sought, as without this, unless a person is already conversant with the subject depicted, its size may be a matter of guess-work. Since the first aim of archaeological photography is to make a full scientific record, the photograph, however good it may be in other ways, is a wasted effort if it does not give some exact indication of size. Trees, buildings and other natural or artificial objects may chance to give a rough indication of the size of the archaeological subject, but even these do not give an exact scale since they vary widely in size themselves. Therefore, all photographs taken for archaeological purposes *must have an accurate scale*. The photographs may possibly go to remote corners of the world; they will be seen by people thousands of miles from the site, and there is a need for more than mere estimates of size; an *absolute* scale in feet and inches, metres and centimetres must be included as part of the picture.

The problem is to introduce the scale in such a position that it is unobtrusive and yet there to be used. Again, it is impossible to lay down a set of rules, but the matter of the scale should be approached bearing in mind that, whilst the main purpose of the picture is scientific, there need be no conflict between science and pictorial sense. The scale should be in proportion to the subject. A small find *in situ* requires a small scale (perhaps a 10-cm. scale) and a large general view might include survey poles with feet painted alternately black and white. Where there is any distance in the subject three of these at least should be included, one in the foreground, one in the middle distance and one in the far distance. The reason for this is that the scale of a photograph alters with the distance from the camera.

Various types of scale may be employed. Small scales can be ruled on a piece of card, with the divisions into inches and centimetres outlined in Indian ink, about two or three inches long overall. A larger subject would require a scale in proportion of the same type, of perhaps 4–6 inches. In a medium close-up on the site the scale could be a square rod of wood about two feet long giving one division of one foot, with the rest in inch markings, alternately black and white. For a wall, ditch or biggish structure the 2-ft. scale would be replaced by a survey pole, which is generally 6 or 8 feet long, the foot divisions painted red, black and white in succession. Much-used survey poles become scratched and the paint chipped. In photographs this shows up very badly and looks untidy so a good scheme, no matter how small the excavation, is to keep at least one survey pole for photographic purposes only, and none but the photographer should be allowed to handle it. The specially allotted pole should be kept, when not in use, in some sort of sheath, to protect it in transit from place to place.

In the general views, a larger area may be shown which will require as many as three survey poles, or it may be found more interesting to introduce a human figure. If this is done, then the figure must seem to be employed, shovel or pick in hand, never just standing idly, gazing at the camera. The human scale-substitute must never look directly at the camera, and should always stand in a working pose, the attitude moderately comfortable (but not too restful) because it may have to be held during a fairly long exposure.

With earthworks, banks and ditches, it is as well to use two, or even three, figures if the distance warrants it – one, say, at the bottom of the ditch, one halfway up the bank, and one at the top of the bank. The figure at the top of the bank should have dark clothing to contrast with the light sky; those not in silhouette should be dressed in lighter tones (e.g. shirt-sleeved), which will show them in contrast to the dark earth. In every case, whether the scale is a survey pole, human figure or small black-and-white scale, it should be so placed as to allow it to become part of the picture, but not obtrusively so that it is the first thing to catch the eye.

Manufacture of the smaller scales is quite simple and they are best made by photographs, as follows. Generally, I have one drawn four times larger than actual size. This is in order to get clear, sharp corners and edges and good lettering. (Lettering, especially, is not simple at an actual size of, say, 6 inches.) The $\times 4$ scale is then photographed down to correct size on process film and from the negative can be made as many prints on a strong contrast *matt* paper as may be needed.

Prints are mounted on thin cardboard and finally trimmed square. Since scales of two, three or four inches are often useful the prints are made six inches long, when they may be cut to a size commensurate with the subject. The scales are stored until required in a holder or a box, so that they keep clean and flat.

One important point. If a survey pole is the scale, it should always stand perfectly vertical in the photograph. If the camera is pointing downwards, looking into a ditch or section, the pole must be adjusted to make it appear upright in the picture. This is done by tipping it at an angle (without moving it from its position in the section) until it appears upright on the ground-glass screen of the camera. Even on level ground, with the camera base perfectly horizontal, great care must be taken to ensure that poles are truly vertical. The adjusting of the poles is best done at the last moment and checked by the photographer on the camera screen.

As well as a number of scales, there will be other small equipment which can be of great use in the field. A stick or two of chalk may be used to dust over iron finds in poor condition to make them show up. Plasticine is used for propping up potsherds and for many other purposes. A stock of pins, drawing-pins, a small pair of scissors to cut any overlooked 'whiskers' that may show, a penknife, a spoon, a 2-in. panel brush and a couple of camel-hair brushes should be carried. They all help in the final cleaning before exposure. These items I keep with my small scales in a box, which goes into the leather camera case containing all my field equipment. To possess a 'box of bits' of this nature is most helpful when one is away from H.Q. and a final touching-up is necessary. The items are easily assembled and if boxed, as suggested, become an essential part of one's equipment.

8

WORK UPON THE SITE

Having a practical working knowledge of the material and being familiar with all the working parts of the camera we can begin work upon the site. Ideally, the photographer should reach the site before work on it has begun, so that he can go round taking a considerable number of general views. This is a wise precaution because frequently, after the ground has been gridded or trenched, it is felt that a view of a particular area before excavation would have been desirable. Once the ground has been disturbed this opportunity is lost for good. If it is at all possible, therefore, it is best for the photographer to make all necessary pictures of the unexcavated site at the very outset. Some of the photographs should be purely pictorial.

It will not be possible to complete this in one day on account of the changing light, but at least one or two views can be recorded safely before the actual marking-out of the excavation begins. As marking-out starts, it might be a good plan to photograph the work in progress, and again when turf has been removed and a little more is to be seen. Because of moving figures some of these shots will have to be done with the shutter so that there must be enough light to give a full exposure at the necessary shutter-speed. These negatives should be developed immediately, and the viewpoint or orientation of each should be noted so that as soon as the negatives are dry they can be registered. It is better to get this registration done immediately a satisfactory print has been made. If left until later there is danger that it may be overlooked.

Assuming that work has now begun, there will, on a large excavation, be other sites, trenches and areas to be treated in the same way and this is where the initial observation of light and possible viewpoint will prove to have been worth while, enabling this part of the recording to be fitted in with the rest of the work. Generally it is customary to photograph the work as it proceeds; that is to say, after the removal of the turf the underlying layer is sometimes cleaned up and photographed. Where the grid system is in use and there are anything from nine to twelve squares laid out, covering a considerable area of ground, it will be found that the best point of view is pretty high – much higher than the fullest extension of the tripod will allow.

For such occasions it is essential to have some method of raising the viewpoint sufficiently, and this can only be done by having a strong stand or platform on which camera and operator can stand. If the cost will allow it, and if there is a prospect of several seasons' work, it would pay to have a portable high platform or grandstand specially constructed. It can, of course, be made so that it is easily taken to pieces and stored against another excavation. If the cost is felt to be too high, a visit to the local village or town might result in the discovery of a builder who is willing to lend or hire out trestles and boards. It is as well, when borrowing such equipment, to ensure that it is all strong and in good condition; for instance, the ropes holding the spread of the trestles must be sound because they have to take the weight of the camera and operator, and work upon these trestles often has to be carried out in quite a high wind.

As a luxury I once enjoyed the use of an electric-light company's portable stand. It had a platform and a railing round it and could be raised with convenience to a height of 36 feet. At the other end of the scale, I have on occasion made the best of half-a-dozen Tate sugar boxes and a few planks. The great thing in such a case is to get well above the subject and this often calls for some ingenuity in out-of-the-way places where ladders and trestles are hard to come by and difficult to transport. There is little use in photographing a grid system without being able to get some way above it. To include such a large area from ground-level would, in any case, mean the use of a wide-angle lens and this would considerably distort the grids in the foreground.

Whilst dealing with the grid system a word may be said on cleanliness. Usually the excavated soil has to be 'barrowed away' and in the course of a day's barrowing and general work the turf suffers much from spill, and wear and tear of many feet. Most site supervisors have the turf and turf balks brushed at the close of a day's work, but a photographer on the site will be very wise to see that this is in fact carried out daily, because it will be the means of a considerable saving of time when preparing for photography. With its daily brush-up the grass has a chance to recover and keep its freshness. In this way it will show well in a photograph provided, of course, that it is kept well cut, particularly at the edges. There must be a pair of garden shears on the site to trim the edges and give them a clean line against the dark earth. This, of course, applies to the large general view of the grids, but there will also be photographic work to do centring round only one or two of the squares. It will be found that one can work from the turf balk for photographs of structures exposed in the squares, such as stone-formation and hearths, all of which must naturally have received the fullest cleaning.

5. *THE NECESSITY FOR A HIGH VIEWPOINT. The first example was taken at eye-level, the second from 15ft. above the ground. The third photograph was taken from 28ft. above the ground, and gains greatly in clarity and informativeness. Note also the clean, well-brushed baulks and clean-cut edges in the two lower pictures.*

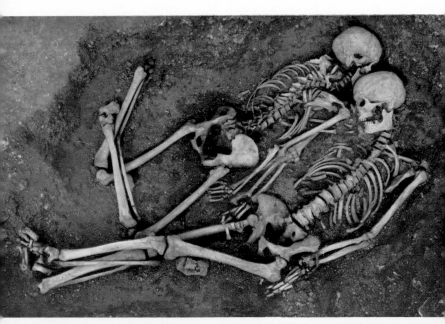

6. *A COLOUR SEPARATION PROBLEM. It is not easy to show up brown bones on dark earth. These two illustrations give examples of correctly cleaned skeletal remains with all earth removed from eye sockets, rib bones, and pelvis, and all bones thoroughly washed and dried. They are then photographed with a camera vertically over the skeletons. (F.32. 20 secs. Tricolour red filter. Sky overcast.)*

With the grid system the dump for excavated soil is some way off and causes no trouble – at least from the photographer's point of view! – but in trenches, with the dump alongside, the earth should be thrown well back, at least 2 ft. 6 in. from the edge of the cut. There is a purpose in this: apart from considerations of safety for the workers, who can use a wide space between dump and cut, earth from a dump that is too close to the edge of the cut will, during a rainstorm, be washed back into the trench. With the dump well back, sweeping and trimming the edge of the dump in preparation for photography is a comparatively simple matter taking very little of the labourer's time; one that reaches the edge of the cut can be a perfect nightmare for all concerned.

For photography of the section in one side of a trench the viewpoint must first be settled, so that, taking into account the field of view of the lens to be used, the cleaning of the section may extend well beyond its limits. With a properly sited dump it is only necessary to brush the turf with a bass broom and trim with the shears as much of the grass edge of the trench as will appear in the picture.

The face of the section must now be prepared. If it is dry it may be freshened by taking off the barest shaving all over with a trowel. Earth photographs much better when slightly damp than when the face is dry and dusty. It is best to work from the top downwards, so that nothing falls on the part already cleaned. The cleanings fall to the bottom of the trench and are shovelled up completely at the very last.

Having freshened up the section it is necessary to consider how best to show up the stratification. If there is plenty of colour contrast in the section, then the material and the light-filter (see pp. 32–35) will handle it satisfactorily, but if the colours of the layers are not distinctive, some 'retouching' must be carried out, since each archaeologically distinct layer

D

has to be distinguishable in the photograph. Differences of texture will sometimes be sufficient, as for example between a deposit full of stones and one without, but it is often necessary, where both texture and colour are nearly the same, to divide one layer from another by slightly undercutting, so that the overhanging base of the upper may cast a slight shadow and so show where one layer ends and another begins. A deep gash is ugly and unnecessary. It is simple to work with the flat of the trowel on the face of the section, taking off just enough with the point to give that little shadow.

The slight undercutting can be repeated when the cleaning of the layers has reached the natural. Where there is little distinction in colour between the last layer and the natural the trowel can be run along the natural, held flat but with its point taking out sufficient of the layer above to cast a slight shadow.

To save time and labour, trenches are not always cut very wide. Photographing the stratification in a narrow trench is extremely difficult and often the only possible viewpoint is at one end of the section. It would be ideal, of course, to have the camera square to the face of the section, but this is not always possible, however wide the trench may be, so whether the trench is wide or narrow the aim must be to obtain as square as possible a view of the face and to get as near as is practicable to its midpoint. This means that the camera must be fairly low, because the whole depth of the section must be visible. A higher viewpoint would mean that the camera would be looking down on to the section, and since most work on stratification has to be done with a fairly short-focus lens, an unnecessarily high viewpoint will cause considerable distortion. Layers in the foreground, although possibly equal in thickness to others further from the camera, have a tendency to be exaggerated.

The adjustment of a survey pole has been described in Chapter 7. The pole must be upright in the picture and may well look askew in the actual subject. Directions will have to be given to an assistant to make this adjustment, while the photographer watches the effect on his focussing screen.

As with the general and pictorial views of earthworks, banks and ditches, the bubble level must always be used to give a true horizontal. Camera routine must include the automatic use of the level. The true horizon is essential if recording is to be accurate. Whether the bubble is applied to the front of the camera or the back is of no consequence. For preference I work with the back of the camera pushed in slightly, leaving just sufficient room to place the level. Its being at the back saves hand movements and makes the level more easily visible during routine camera adjustments, since all the adjusting screws are also at the back.

9

THE TREATMENT OF
BRICK, STONE AND PLASTER WALLS

In the photographic treatment of walls, whether of brick, stone or plaster, the utmost cleanliness of the subject is essential. When first excavated, stone walls still have some soil or mud adhering to the mortar coursing. If this is very wet it should be allowed to dry. If the wall is in a good state of repair it can be brushed until every grain of earth has been removed. The best kind of brush to use is that usually employed in dairy work. One brush, at least, should always be kept for the final brushing-up before the photograph is taken. A stone wall should sparkle!

Experience has proved that, if the light is suitable, the early morning, just before the dew has dried, will be the best time to expose. Stonework then has some depth of colour, which is an advantage, always provided that the dampness is not patchy. Again, choice of the best light can only be made after watching, waiting and immediately seizing the opportunity as it presents itself.

Unlike plaster, stone walls do not need to be kept continually damp. Plastered walls of Roman buildings, with their lined decoration at chair-rail height and the coloured corner moulding, are often a little grey or dull when dry. After thoroughly cleaning or just before the actual exposure it may be helpful to wipe them over with a damp rag or, if the surface is friable, with a brush dipped in water. Should the water, which is intended to give depth to the colours, dry too quickly, a small amount of glycerine added to it and well stirred will hold the moisture for a little longer.

On some sites brick walls, brick herringbone pavements, brick or tile courses are common. When just excavated, earth clings to the joints between the bricks, and this must be moved before attempting to take a photograph. Prolonged cleaning with a stiffish brush to remove every particle of loose earth is the only way. With brickwork the lighting chosen will depend mainly upon the wall construction. Sometimes the courses are separated by thick beds of mortar. Such a wall will not require lighting at too acute an angle to its face, but with mud-brick walls, where the courses are not so distinct, the lighting will have to be extremely sharp in order to show up each course.

The preliminary treatment of herringbone pavements is the same as for brick and tile course, i.e. stiff brushing and the removal of soil from the interstices. The lighting will have to be different. It is a low light that is needed, coming at a sharp angle to the horizontal. Counter-light (see p. 37), with the lens pointing towards the light source, throws up the shadows cast by the edges of the bricks. The lens will have to be shielded in that case, but this should present no difficulty because the camera will certainly be tipped to look down a little. There are no particular points of difficulty with the camera in photographing walls. If they are of any considerable height the uprights will have to be watched. If the short-focus or wide-angle lens is used the side-swing of the camera can be adjusted to obtain perfect definition. Avoid, if possible, too sharp a perspective.

It is better to take too many pictures of a plastered wall subject than too few. Unless it is highly decorated a plaster wall is rarely removed and most are re-buried when filling in. Exposures from several angles should be made, making sure that at the end of the excavation the connections of the subject with surrounding structures appear in at least two of the photographs. For scale, use a survey-pole in the case of a length of wall. Suitable smaller foot or inch scales will be included should a detail photograph be required.

Portions of paved roads, or roads made up with pebbles, require a tremendous amount of cleaning – particularly the latter. These can give a most pleasing result when well washed, but it may take at least four washings to get a pebble-surface clean. The simplest way (providing the road is in good condition) is to tip a bucket of water over it and brush with a large bass broom, just as in washing down a stable. Plenty of water and energy are required to prepare a picture of this kind which really means something. Once clean, use a counter-light for such a subject, fairly low.

Sometimes it may be necessary to cut a section of the roadway to show how it was repaired or rebuilt in ancient times. This should be treated like other sections – well brushed to show the significant layers and periods of repair, with a clean, sharp angle where the section ends on the natural, the foundation on which the road was first built.

10

EARTH SECTIONS AND STRATIFICATION

As a photographer specializing in archaeological subjects, earth and soils interest me intensely – not so much for their archaeological meaning as for their texture and for what may be done to make them register this special character in the emulsion. Every time I prepare a section for photography, I meet with a variety of soils: sticky soils, friable soils, the tough boulder-clay soil with small lumps of chalk in it, sandy soil or pure yellow clay. It is perhaps the familiarity born only of long association, but the moment my trowel bites into them I feel I know their photographic requirements.

Two rather interesting soil sections come to mind. The first was in the very early days of my association with archaeology. In a rampart-section appeared some turves, used as a revetment to the bank in some ancient period of construction or reconstruction. These were like patches of black clay in the section. The earth embedding them was of exactly the same colour and, although the texture was somewhat different, photographically I could not obtain a good separation between the decayed turves and their surroundings. Whilst waiting for a favourable light I was playing with the material and, running the pads of my fingers over it, discovered that it would take a polish. I therefore began to polish up the surfaces of all the turves, without touching the surrounding earth. Another exposure was made and although my polishing did show, the distinction which it gave was still not bold enough to tell the story properly. On the following day, preparing for another attempt, I dropped the lens cap into the trench and, after jumping down to retrieve it, looked up and noticed that the 'fossil' turves were shining with light reflected from the sky. Instead of approaching the section at right angles, therefore, I photographed it at a rather acute angle, so that the polished turves, catching the light, stood out from their background in an extremely pleasing manner. This was one of those simple things, so simple that it was surprising not to have thought of it earlier. I did not fully appreciate at the time how much could be done with the soil itself to improve a photograph.

Sections in the soil are vitally important in archaeology, but nearly always form the most difficult of subjects. There may be little difference in colour, and not a great deal in texture, that lends itself to the making of a telling photograph. There is a regular code of practice in cutting these sections. The shallower cuts, up to eight feet deep, have sides strictly vertical, while in those up to twenty feet the sides are usually cut back at a slight angle, or 'batter'. This is for reasons of safety and may enable the excavators to dispense with the shoring otherwise necessary in a deep vertical-sided trench. Sections cut to a batter are generally very well illuminated, particularly if the trench is a wide one, but with the shallower, but narrow, trench, lighting the face becomes a problem. The main object in obtaining the picture of a section is to distinguish between the various layers, and this is very largely achieved by accentuating the changes in texture, in one way or another. The exact treatment must vary with the textures encountered in the particular section.

My second most interesting section subject was a rubbish pit, the filling of which, if I remember rightly, was cut through by the main section. The pit itself was about fifteen feet deep and contained a certain amount of pottery, the texture of the filling being of a very porous nature, lightly packed. It was about five feet wide, narrowing to three feet at the base, and had been cut through various layers. There was little variation in colour, but many varying textures. The treatment devised was to trim the whole face down vertically, the sealing layer left untouched but the layers to each side of the pit *cut back* slightly, so that the filling stood out in slight relief. The layers cut by the walls of the pit were undercut in order to give the slight shadow previously referred to. Since the textures of these layers were so varied, i.e. sandy, clayey and mixed soils, nothing was needed beyond a discreet polishing of the most clayey parts. The whole was brushed free of dust, left overnight and photographed the following morning, when all it required was minor cleaning of the floor and the angles of the cut. Practice with the various types of soil found in these sections will soon teach by experience the particular treatment for each kind of layer.

Let us now exchange sticky black earth for chalk – lovely to work in and to photograph. When properly clean it sparkles. The floor of an excavation is generally cleaned by scraping, when here and there the muddy crust flakes away, leaving a clean white surface. While damp, it is fairly easy to clean, but once dry it becomes more difficult, as is the case with limestone. Once cleaned of earth, continual hard scraping with a trowel will enable it to dry out clean and sparkling – an ideal subject for photography. When working on limestone, if it rains overnight and the morning sees little puddles in the depressions, mop them dry as one would water that has been slopped on a floor. The dirt sediment that has settled from these pools must then be scraped off and the surface be allowed to dry. Even if the photograph is not to be taken that day or hour, mop up puddles and scrape, so that the surface is kept to a uniform colour and does not have that patchy, mottled appearance which shows up so badly on a photograph.

We seem to have returned to the subject of cleanliness! The best way to achieve it is to clean up as much as possible as one proceeds, sharpening edges, cutting to a clean angle while the earth is still damp and soft. While actually excavating, consideration should be given to the way in which the work in hand will be photographed, and to that end the brushing of stones, and undercutting to get slight shadows, can well be done as the work proceeds. It leaves so much less to be done when the time comes to take the photographs. There is less to think about and more time to concentrate on the correct angle, focus, the light and so on.

Lastly, all irrelevancies and 'clutter' must be removed from the field of view. Among such things are trays or tools left on the edge of the cut, oddments of clothing hanging on nearby trees, planks lying untidily at all angles, forgotten barrows and buckets still to be seen in the middle distance. Once more, consider the grass at the edge – is it cut right back? Pick up any fallen leaves that may have blown into the excavation since its final cleaning. Exclude or move the site desk and the human figure that is just visible on the edge of the picture.

Since a section is generally cut vertically and the laws of photography call for parallel planes, the camera should stand as square to the sections as possible. Sections are mostly exposed in more or less deep trenches, so that it is essential to get the camera as low as possible, even to resting it on the turf. If there is a likelihood of there being much of this work, it pays to have a suitable box or pillar made, on which the camera can be fixed a few inches from the ground.

It is realized that the subject of sections has only been lightly touched. It is impossible to give a general rule. Some sections are only exposed in fairly narrow trenches, some are through a mound or hillock of which half has been cut completely away. Others appear when work is well advanced and very deep down. Each resolves itself into a small colour problem, and should be so considered, in the light of our known standards – (a) the sensitivity of the photographic material, (b) its response to the different types of filter, and the degree of contrast it will give when correctly exposed and developed.

11

SKELETAL REMAINS

Not infrequently archaeological excavations unearth human remains. From a photographer's standpoint there is very little difficulty with skeletal remains beyond the proper cleaning of the bones. The position in which a skeleton is lying sometimes poses a problem of lighting or angle, but in the main it is the cleaning which takes the time and is the most important. The actual taking of the photograph then resolves itself into another colour-separation problem.

Different kinds of soil seem to affect the remains in various ways. In my experience the usual black occupation soil does not seem to soften bones very much. Care and gentle handling are obviously necessary but if the bones are in reasonably good condition they will bear the cleaning treatment very well. Bones in chalky soils are generally well preserved.

Remains in coffins are the most difficult to clean, principally because of the awkward position in which they are found, but also because it is necessary to clean round the coffin as well as inside it. In the case of the average skeleton found by a wall or in a ditch (provided it is not waterlogged) or a burial in a field, there is a fair amount of room in which to work comfortably. The earth round the bones can be easily removed and the cleaning can be done as excavation progresses. At the very last the soil round the pelvis, in the eye sockets, and the angles formed by folded limbs must be carefully removed with a spoon, having first been loosened with a penknife or other pointed tool. In small crevices, as between the vertebrae and among the ribs, the earth may be brushed away with a 1-in. panel paint brush. Every care must be taken to avoid any disturbance of their original position. It is a good plan to regard the bones as 'teed up' like a golf ball. Thus they are undercut as much as possible having regard, of course, to leaving proper support so that they stand out from the surrounding earth sufficiently to be in high relief. It is a waste of time to clear only just enough earth to show the bones as a pattern on a flat surface, like an inlay; the relief is important.

Having cleaned the remains as much as may be, the next thing to do is to wash the bones with a panel brush and clean water frequently. The excess of water will be absorbed by the earth on which the bones lie. If circumstances permit, the whole subject should be allowed to dry, the washed bones assuming a lighter colour when dry than when first unearthed. This is an advantage for photography, because the bones now stand out from their background and greater contrast is obtained.

Camera position can now be arranged. Sometimes two shots are necessary: one in an oblique direction to show the depth of the remains below the turf or to fix their position in relation to other features of the site or section, another with the camera vertically over the skeleton. The selection of the appropriate light filter will depend on the colour of the bones. If they are very brown, then with the panchromatic material, a deep red or tricolour red should be used. For a lighter, yellow-brown colour the yellow filter would be used. The effect in both cases would be to make the bones appear light against a dark background. The filter passes the reddish-browns while the dark earth reflects but little light in the red-yellow region and remains black. The multiplying factor of the filter used must always be borne in mind and allowed for.

As to the use of scales, there is a great variety of practice. In Great Britain, I have rarely used a scale with an average adult skeleton of which the dimensions are well known. With a skeleton of unusual size it would be advisable and it is absolutely necessary with infant or child burials. For such skeletons as I have photographed overseas, I have never used more than the two shots, one for fixing the position of the body and one vertically to record the attitude and details of the skeleton. I have, however, worked with some overseas negatives which had two scales on every vertical photograph of a skeleton: one lying along the skeleton and another at right angles to it forming a letter L. In addition these photographs had in the field a large card giving the sex, the orientation, and the serial number of the grave as well. While extremely efficient technically, this, to my mind, did distract attention from the subject.* In the case of a whole cemetery, the photographer, having photographed the remains, would check the details of each burial with the site supervisor and record them both on his negative and in his negative register. On system in recording more will be said later.

Skeletal remains found in chalk provide photographic conditions which are the reverse of the last problem. Instead of contrasting reddish-brown with black, on chalk, bones are

---

*I have been informed by Dr Cornwall, who was at one time working on the publication of the material found in the graves referred to, that the incorporation of the grave-numbers in the photograph was often invaluable in identifying objects which, through the passage of years and frequent handling, had lost labels or other marks of provenance. The negative itself was in some cases the only clue, since the details in the register were often inadequate.

in the main relatively dark on a light background. Here, an orthochromatic emulsion could easily be used to obtain the necessary contrast, but a similar result can be realized by the use of panchromatic emulsion and a deep-green filter, which will hold back the reds while passing yellows. Since the bones are on a white background, the desired contrast should be obtained.

Sand is perhaps the worst of all soils in which to find remains. While preliminary cleaning is easy, colour-contrasts are difficult to obtain and one is often compelled to rely entirely on light to give relief. The brushing away of sand from the bones is simple, provided that there is no wind, and very little washing is necessary. Because of wind-drifted sand it is best to photograph immediately after cleaning, for if the subject has to be left the whole process of brushing will have to be repeated.

Close-up details of any unusual features in human remains, such as trephined skulls, broken or diseased bones, details of jewellery and decoration, should be photographed in addition to the general views of a burial for the record. When photographing these details it must be remembered that there will have to be an increase in exposure owing to the close-up position and it may, further, be necessary to stop down, perhaps to F.32 or even F.64, in order to get perfect definition; this will require additional exposure-time.

Sometimes, when cleaning, a little too much earth is removed and a bone slips out of its original position. A piece of plasticine from the 'bits box' (Chapter 7) may be moulded and placed under the bone, but out of sight, to prop it in position. Other items in the box may also be useful here, among them the camel-hair paint-brush and the spoon as a miniature dust-pan for last-minute removal of dirt and dust before the exposure is made.

Finally, it must be borne in mind that in the finished result the attitude of the burial, whether crouched or extended, must be clear from the first glance at the photograph ; there must be no distortion. If possible, therefore, the lens of longest focal length must be used and, in the vertical photograph, the lens must be accurately over the centre of the burial and the back of the camera centred behind it.

The 'tipping head' to the tripod will be used for the verticals, but occasions sometimes present themselves when the burials are found in trenches that are deep and narrow, when it is impossible to have the tripod in the trench. In such a case the only thing to do is to have planks bridging the trench and to stand the outfit on them. Preferably use double planks (one on top of the other) to make the bridge rigid. The exposure is likely to be pretty long if the remains are at any depth and a filter and small stop are being used. A steady platform reduces the chance of jarring during exposure. Whilst single planks may be perfectly safe, the absence of any 'whip' with the double set gives an added sense of security when working.

7. *TERRAIN AND LIGHT used to show up a well defended entrance.*

8. *RIGHT AND WRONG.* Above: *Evening shadows give depth and shape to the picture. Noonday sun (below) makes it flat and lifeless.*

9. *MAKESHIFT DARKROOMS. In a Breton wash-house* (above) *the dry side was a board on a ladder covered with clean paper. The dry side in the Normandy wine-cellar* (below) *is divided by a partition from the wet.*

12

MOSAIC PAVEMENTS

Each type of archaeological site has its own potentialities according to the period and culture to which it belongs. On a Roman villa site, therefore, it is quite possible that a mosaic pavement may be uncovered. Should this be the case, it is a feature that will have to be photographed very fully, from the first discovery of some tesserae in position to the lifting of the pavement, if that is eventually undertaken. Even if the pavement is only a small one, the fullest possible record should always be made of it, because if it seems worthy neither of permanent preservation on the spot, nor of lifting and removal to a museum, it will be covered once more when the excavation is filled in.

The moment for the first photograph is the moment when the first corner is uncovered, when the picture should show its position and relationship to the whole building. As the work proceeds and more earth is removed, further photographs are taken at intervals until the final clearing. The first few will most likely be oblique views taking in all necessary details of the surroundings, but the final shot should be a vertical photograph. Every effort must be made to take this last shot truly vertically, not only because it will look better in that view, but because the later detailed study of the mosaic from photographs is thus made easier. It is practically impossible to obtain an exact scale from an oblique photo-

E

graph unless one is in possession of the 'taking' data, such as the focal length of the lens, height of the camera from the ground and so on. Even so, not every archaeologist knows how to do it and measuring and sketching the design will be more accurate when working from a vertical photograph, provided that it is on a stated scale, preferably a simple fraction, such as $\frac{1}{4}$ or $\frac{1}{18}$ of the actual size of the subject.

In the larger pavements the decoration, apart from 'guilloche', 'key' and other formal patterns, sometimes has panels depicting scenes. Each of these should be photographed separately, as should also any unusual irregularity in pattern or difference in execution which may indicate where repairs in ancient times were carried out.

The most difficult part of photographing a pavement is to get the camera well above it. This normally means scaffolding, which should always be erected by competent workmen, trained in scaffold erection. It need not be very heavy, as long as it will take the weight of the operator and his equipment.

Another but perhaps less satisfactory method is to photograph a large pavement in sections, which can later be joined together into a single picture. Before beginning photography the pavement should be 'lined out' with white string in strips of the width of the field included by the lens, when the camera will have to be moved between a number of exposures along each strip, until the whole area has been covered. One essential in carrying out a piece of work like this is to clamp the camera after focusing on the first section and never to touch that setting until the job is finished. If one section is out of scale the whole series is completely ruined. It must also be borne in mind that as long as the distance from lens to plate is fixed, the distance from lens to pavement must never be altered.

In a long series of photographs of this nature the choice of light is all-important. It is best, if possible, to choose a dull sort of day when the light, if not perfect, is likely to be steady. It must be remembered that a large number of negatives may have to be made and too much variation between them in exposure will mean variation in print-quality. A recent task of this nature that I undertook, the recording of the superb pavement at Lullingstone, Kent, required 40 negatives. I started early and finished late, the exposures, checked each time, varying from 10 seconds at the start of the day to $2\frac{1}{2}$ minutes at the close.

Lighting a mosaic pavement requires a great deal of care. Experience has shown that strong sunlight is too harsh, particularly with close-up details. The shadows thrown into the interstices between the tesserae spoil the appearance of the pavement and make the work seem coarser than it really is. Full sunlight, moreover, will give more or less deep shadows where the pavement has sunk, with corresponding highlights on the remaining eminences. Under no circumstances can the photographer rely even on a diffused light to conceal all unevennesses and the successful treatment of pavements in this condition requires experience and some skill. Providing the scale for a pavement is fairly simple. With a large pavement a horizontal survey pole is suitable, well to one side and off the actual pattern, lying on the red brick tesserae surrounding the pavement proper. For detail pictures a scale commensurate with the size of the work is needed, having sub-divisions of feet or metres appropriate to the area in the field of view. In the progress-photographs a vertical pole might be included to give the depth of the pavement below turf line.

The cleaning of a pavement before photography can be a major undertaking. Where the surface is only muddy or

dusty, brushes or cloths and not too much water are indicated, since the water is inclined to loosen the tesserae. Where
the building was destroyed by fire there may be burnt
patches on the pavement. Soot and firing can be removed
gradually with Vim or wet silver sand, but burnt areas may
be permanently discoloured. After washing and drying the
colours in a pavement often look a trifle dull from a photographic standpoint. It is advisable slightly to damp the pavement just before exposing to bring up the colours. The area
included in the angle of view may be wiped over with a
cloth wrung out in clean water, and if the exposure threatens
to be very long so that the surface dries patchily, a little
glycerine should be added to the water. While the tesserae
are moist the colours will have a depth which will give
better contrasts.

There are often several minor colours in a pavement
besides the white background – red, yellow and blue pre-
dominating together with varying shades of these colours. It
is obvious that treatment with a too vigorous contrast-filter
would 'kill' some colours and so give a mistaken impression
of the design. A filter must be chosen which will not spoil
finer gradations of colour in the work but which will, at the
same time, slightly darken any pale blues, which are easily
lost. Using a yellow filter and panchromatic emulsion it will
be found that the gradations and colours appear of the same
tonal value as that seen by the eye.

There are, of course, many other finds which call for
photography during an excavation though they may not be
as exciting as a pavement or a rich burial. If not shown they
are on the whole more valuable, because more common, and
on them will be based important archaeological conclusions.
'Finds in situ' are likely to be of vital importance and therefore call for close attention. They also demand especially

careful cleaning, and faultless lighting, focusing and exposure. Generally, because of their delicate condition, there
will be only one chance of photographing them *in situ*. As
soon as the photograph is taken they are lifted; seldom can
they be left exposed, even overnight, to the elements, for
fear that they might break up.

When such groups or deposits of weapons, pots etc. are
found, it is wise to obtain a photograph immediately. As
ever, scrupulous cleanliness is of chief importance. The careful removal of a proportion of the surrounding earth is
necessary in order that all of the finds may stand out in relief.
It must be remembered that nothing may be removed or
shifted, so that painstaking and careful excavation will be
required. If, after this cleaning has been done, the subject
appears still to be absorbed by the background, a light dust-
ing of the finds on the shaded side with a finger previously
rubbed with chalk will be found to help in giving contrast.

For the photograph, the light or time at which the subject
is best shown must be selected. It is obvious that if the relief
of the finds is shallow the light-direction will need to be low
if good light and shade are to be obtained (an early-morning
or late-evening light). If the subject has high relief then the
light must be less oblique. In both cases it is essential to watch
lest the shadow of one object should fall upon and obscure
another. On occasion a counter-light, i.e. working with the
camera facing towards the sun, may be of assistance. This, as
always, will require careful shading of the lens, in order that
the light may not fall directly on the lens and so fog the plate.
If a vertical position of the camera is required, the tipping
head will be brought into play. Where time and material
allow, it is well to have, not only the vertical photographs,
but also an oblique view, which should show the relation of
the particular area of the finds to the rest of the excavation.

A scale proportioned to the object or area must be included in this view.

Finds *in situ* may sometimes consist of pieces of textiles, leather, basket-work, burnt wheat, all of which are difficult to clean. Well cleaned they must be, nevertheless, because this may be the only possible photograph, should they be spoiled in lifting. In such a case as this, it is best to take two or three views of the subject, varying the exposure and the position of the camera. If the light is too one-sided on such a subject, the shadows can be relieved by the reflection from a piece of white card or a board covered with silver foil. There is nothing very difficult in improving the shadows in this way. I have used the method of reflection on subjects lying at the bottom of a deep trench, but care must be taken that the light, thus equalized, does not make the subject too flat and uninteresting.

Panchromatic material will be used, possibly with a filter, if it is thought necessary to obtain contrast or separation of colours, where colours exist. Some black subjects such as leather or burnt wheat will, in all probability, catch the light and shine a little. This is to the good, for such reflections will help to pick out details against the unreflecting dark earth. Subjects like the remains of ovens, ghost-walls or sleeper beams, each require individual treatment, so that it becomes impossible to lay down a general rule to cover every contingency. In all cases, the utmost cleanliness, cleaning extending well beyond the area viewed by the lens, a level horizon, and sufficient shading of the lens to cut out any extraneous light, are indispensable.

Exposure may be gauged either by meter or by experience. The latest form of light-meter (not prohibitively expensive to most pockets) now records some light-value, even in the deepest shadow. Archaeological photography calls for vast differences in exposure between one subject and another. If a trench is taken, for example, the light at the turf-line is brilliant, but the amount of light at the bottom of the trench, where the last archaeological layer and the natural have to be well exposed, is at the other end of the scale. Exposure must always be for the bottom of the trench in accordance with a rule originating many years ago: 'Expose for the shadows and let the highlights take care of themselves.'

13

OTHER WORK UPON THE SITE

For a moment, let us leave the field and consider a few of the tasks a photographer might meet at 'H.Q.'. The variety of these tasks is multiplied according to the size of the site and the number of seasons it will be worked.

Once having built a darkroom or adapted a room to serve, a multiplicity of jobs will present themselves. Small finds represent only one item. A proportion of these often has to be left behind on overseas excavations, so it is essential to get first-class photographs of them. If the excavation can afford it, there should be a second camera to be used solely for work of this nature. The field camera would, of course, do, but often just as it has been set up for a delicate task at H.Q. it may be urgently required on the site. If so, time is wasted by interrupting the task in hand in order to dash out with the camera. In these circumstances a special camera at H.Q. would be most useful.

The photography of these finds is generally carried out with the camera vertically mounted over a large sheet of ground glass, supported at its edges about two feet from the ground by a box or four pillars. A large sheet of white paper lies on the floor below it. The ground glass should have approximately the same proportions as the size of plate being used. Failing that, an area of the same proportions as the focusing screen may be laid out in pencil on the ground glass. This outlines the display of finds in order that they may fit into the plate. The whole arrangement should be placed facing a north-lighted window, having a blind. By means of the blind it is possible to control the light on the subject: if a sharp edge-light is required, for instance, then the blind is pulled down, and raised again for one less oblique. Any of the site-camera lenses save the wide-angle can be used, since good-quality anastigmats will have been chosen. The finds are duly arranged on the glass, with the help of a T-square and right-angle set-square to ensure orderly arrangement. The top, bottom and sides of the display must always lie true and a scale in balance with the whole must be included.

Ground glass has been specified for supporting the objects. Plain glass can be used, but it does tend to give unwanted reflections in the white paper below, while ground glass gives a clean diffused background. To use plain glass with black paper below means fatal reflections. On this account, if much work is to be done requiring black backgrounds, it is better to use a length of black velvet, tightly stretched over a board, which should have the same proportions as the plate on which the work is being carried out. A point about velvet, however, is that it has to be brushed with the nap each time the subject is changed or marks of the previous arrangement will show.

Generally, with this type of work, it is customary to 'fill up' the plate, hence the necessity of the glass or velvet board being in proportion to the plate. It avoids wastage and promotes a uniform style of presentation.

On occasion, photographs are required at actual size, or some simple fraction of this. This is usual when reproducing drawings of potsherds and finds. Not much work of this sort is done on excavations in Great Britain, but overseas it is more often called for. A good plan when definite dimensions are required is to take the longest dimension that the plate being used will hold. If a whole-plate camera is being used, $7\frac{1}{2}$ in. is as much as can be included with safety. The next thing is to cut a length of paper of which the image can be reduced to $7\frac{1}{2}$ in. when focusing – 15 in. for half-size reduction, 30 in. for quarter-size and so on. The greater the reduction the less is the likelihood of error. When the correct scale has been adjusted the back of the camera should be fixed and never altered until the task is finished. Final focusing is carried out by moving the camera as a whole backwards and forwards.

Before attempting the reproduction of drawings or plans, a good situation must be found that will afford an even light over a long period. It is essential to have a good drawing-board to place in the selected portion on which the drawings can be pinned. The camera, set to the correct scale, is squared up so that its back is in a plane parallel to that of the drawing-board. In the case of black-and-white diagrams process material will be used and a stop of, say, F.16. After exposure, development of the plate should be carried out if possible with a process developer in order that the greatest contrast may result. The negative so obtained should have clear lines, and if laid on a sheet of white paper the work should be visible. Other copying tasks include blueprints consisting of white lines on a blue ground. These can be carried out on panchromatic material with the addition of a red filter. This will 'black out' the blue and leave the white. A minimum exposure with prolonged development should meet the case. I have even had to copy pages from books, both letterpress and illustrations, on a site as part of the day's work, and there is nothing to prevent such a request cropping up again. This is my reason for suggesting that a certain amount of process material should always be carried even in the field. On at least one excavation, I spent days in various museums photographing relevant material ranging from books and plans to objects and potsherds and complete pots. Demand for such odd jobs does arise and it is obvious that they have to be tackled forthwith as a later chance may never occur.

Photography of 'type' pottery may be required either on a 'dig' or even when the photographer is not excavating but just visiting. Procedure is the same in both cases. Occasionally photographs may be wanted of comparative material in the local museum. This is where the small 9×12 cm. camera for 'tip and run' work is useful (Chapter 2).

Extreme care with the background and lighting is necessary. The aim, whether on the excavation or in a museum, is to devise a smooth, contrasting background which will show clearly both the outline of the pot and its lip, belly and base, as well as a form of lighting that will present its features, thumb-nail pattern, incised decoration and texture intelligibly. To photograph either the profile or the surface detail separately is not very difficult. To render both adequately in a single negative requires a certain amount of skill and experience. The pot or group of pots is placed on a sheet of white paper with a white-paper background some two to three feet away, i.e. out of focus. The table on which they stand is moved to secure a suitable light, and heavy shadows are avoided by using a reflector. The background, if even and shadowless, is the making of such a photograph. If the background is full of irrelevant detail the profile of the pot is lost against it and the result is quite valueless. Remember that the background cannot be blocked out. If this has been done the photograph ceases to be an untouched record of the pot. No matter how careful the operator with the brush and bottle of 'opaque', the true shape of the pot cannot be presented. Blocking-out, even when done by the very skilled, is still artificial and the line inevitably shows. In unskilled hands, something totally unlike the original can result. Archaeological photography is like justice – it must not only be done: it must also *appear* to be done. Where background has been blocked out justice *may* have been done, but the result is not above suspicion. Time is better spent in ensuring a good background in the first instance, not forgetting the scale, which must be vertical and in the same plane as the centres of the pots. A thin or a dense negative can be made to give a reasonably good print, but nothing can save a pot on a 'messy' background. These considerations apply whether working on an excavation or visiting museums, whether a large whole-plate camera or a miniature is used.

It was once my fate to 'make good' a series of pot negatives photographed in a hotel bedroom. The exposures were quite good, but the inclusion of a magnificent pair of twin beds in the background and the lack of a scale cost me two full days of work; the result was extremely unscientific and brought little gratification on its completion.

With this kind of work, backgrounds are as important as cleanliness is in the field. Everything can be done without much equipment apart from a first-class camera lens. The background is a matter of common sense in lighting combined with a deal of patience.

The foregoing section applies mainly to complete pots that will stand up and can be placed in a suitable position, but broken potsherds are often of equal or greater importance. These are treated in the same way as the small finds, photographed on a sheet of ground glass, neatly arranged with oblique lighting if they need it. If they are dull and painting and decoration does not show, they may be moistened with clean water and a panel brush. For indistinct ornament in low relief chalk may be brushed into crevices and blown out again: enough will be left to show up the design or pattern if there is any. As on the site or with a section as the subject, all 'retouching' must be done before the exposure.

Large groups of pots do present some little difficulty. If a considerable group is wanted, a large space of white or light-coloured wall or a large sheet of cartridge paper about three to four feet behind the subject will serve as a background. The reason for having the background so far away is that any shadows which may be cast are dispersed and the background remains uniform in tone. Shelves of glass, or wood battens covered with white paper, may be set up, vertically spaced sufficiently to give a fair clearance to the rows. Never omit a clear scale of a size to suit the group.

A final recommendation: a common mistake is to place the camera too close to the subject. The desired view of a single pot or a group is one as near to the true profile ('elevation' an architect would call it) as the camera can give. Thus, the further the camera is (within reason!) from the subject, the nearer is the resulting image to the true profile. The lens of longest focal length in the set comes closest to this ideal.* For the same reason, the viewpoint must be neither too high nor too low. A narrow ellipse visible at the rim of the pot in the middle of the group shows the correct height. Those above this level will be seen slightly from below, those below it slightly from above, but if the camera is well back the departure from true profile, even in the extreme members of the group, will be insignificant.

*If a telephoto lens is available, and there is space to use it, this will give the best result of all. Failing this, exposure with a long-focus lens, followed by enlargement of the central part of the negative, will come very close to a true-profile view of the subject. This is specially desirable in the case of human skulls.

14

THE DARKROOM

The dominant note in these chapters has been, hitherto, the importance of photography in archaeology. I have tried to suggest simplified methods of working so that the operator may almost forget the camera and give his undivided attention to the requirements of the site.

When the plate or film has been exposed, there follows the question of processing it. The best way, on any excavation, even if only of one season's duration, is to develop at once. Overseas, or on sites where there are going to be several seasons' work, it is essential to process and print on the site. Some directors of excavations insist on development immediately after the photograph has been taken, others are content for the photographer to develop daily, still others store up exposures and let the processing wait even longer. My own preference is for immediate developing whenever possible, provided, of course, that the darkroom is easily accessible.

The darkroom must be of easy access: not only easily reached from all parts of the site, but easy to work in with a fair degree of comfort. This is an important point in hot climates. There was a time, even in commercial photography, when the darkroom was just a last-thought 'cubby-hole'. Mercifully, that view has changed and the darkroom, which is the pivotal point in photography, has now No. 1 priority, for it has been seen that better, cleaner work comes out of a good workroom. When an excavation is being planned and the allotment of space for offices and quarters is being designed, attention to darkroom requirements should come high on the list. Choice of site must be governed in the first place by availability of water-supply, either existing or proposed. In the tropics, the position should be one that receives the minimum amount of sun, and the maximum amount of shade, for temperature plays a large part in processing and the coolest available place is the best for the darkroom. Apart from that, the considerations which follow are applicable to darkrooms anywhere.

The room chosen for a darkroom need not be very large, but it must be light-tight. The very best blacking-out is seldom good enough without a very close inspection. When the darkroom is said to be completed, the photographer enters and shuts the door. After allowing a few minutes for the eyes to become accustomed to darkness, cracks admitting light will normally be seen in several places and these will have to be stopped up. A good way to locate them is to take a piece of chalk into the room and, having shut out all obvious light, to mark the cracks with chalk as they appear. Afterwards black paper is pasted over all the chalk marks. The efficiency of this is again tested after waiting in darkness and watching for further leakages of daylight, which must be repaired. The time and trouble spent making the darkroom perfectly light-tight will be well repaid in care-free processing and confidence in the workroom.

Making the room light-tight should be a definite job, whether it is to be used for one season, several seasons, or only for a week. Only on being finally satisfied that the room is light-tight may one proceed to furnish it with tanks, developing dishes and the rest of the equipment.

The room is next theoretically divided into two halves, allowing one half for the *wet* side, the other half for the *dry* side. The position of the boundary between wet and dry halves is of no consequence so long as they are distinct, but the dry end or side must be *kept* dry, i.e. there must be no tanks or dishes or spilt water near. The reason is that, at the dry end, the loading and unloading of the darkslides will take place and the working space allocated to this should be covered with clean brown paper, changed weekly. If, for example, a string is put up on which to hang work to dry, it must not pass over the dry portion, lest the drips from films and prints fall there, when trouble will surely follow.

In the field, one hardly expects ideal conditions, but every effort should be made to obtain the best conditions possible. The wet end of the darkroom should have its tanks, dishes and bottles, and the whole arrangement should be such that as little wet traffic as possible comes near the dry in the rotation of the work.

An important part of the equipment of the darkroom should be a linen or huckaback towel, which should be changed frequently, and a couple of dusters. This may sound like unnecessary elaboration and perhaps even affectation, but I never go on an excavation without my darkroom towels. Clean, dry fingers to handle new material into darkslides are in my opinion an essential. Cleanliness in the darkroom is just as important as on the site.

Failing running water in the darkroom (and I have only had such a luxury twice in a lifetime) have the room as near the water supply as possible. This saves untold time and work. *Never*, NEVER mix developer or hypo in the darkroom. Do it outside and take the solution in. Mixing chemicals in a darkroom is fatal and all sorts of trouble can occur and will be traced to this mistake.

10.   USING THE SKY as a background to dramatize features. Both shots were exposed through a tricolour red filter, aperture F.32.

11. *THE RIGHT POSITION – and there is sometimes only one – can make all the difference between photographing a meaningless jumble of buildings (below) and giving a clear view of their general layout. Both pictures were taken on the same day, the lower one through a deep-yellow filter, the upper, from higher ground, with a tricolour red filter.*

With care, any room or shed, provided it is perfectly light-tight, will make a darkroom, but some forethought as to work-processes and rotation will be a great help. Recently, I chose a room in which to work and blacked it out very thoroughly. When it was finished, I realized for the first time that opening the door in the dark was going to be a problem. It further became clear that a great deal of traffic other than my own was going to pass close by (it was a room within a room). I had even set up my darkroom lights already. Realizing at this point that trouble would be inevitable if I persisted, I cut the loss of three or four hours' hard labour, tore it all down, found another room that promised freedom from all inconveniences and started again. Of course, I had chosen the first room because it was easier to black out. The second choice was admirable, but I suffered a certain amount of inward chagrin for not having given the matter a little more thought in the first place.

I have devised darkrooms under all sorts of conditions and, on the whole, have been able to produce clean work in good time. This would probably not have been the case without my system of dry and wet sides of the room. Cellar or attic, I can only see a darkroom in two parts – Wet and Dry !

Let us now review the work that will have to be carried out in the darkroom. Firstly, the rapid loading of plates or films before the day's work will take place at the dry end, on which our clean paper is spread over the bench. In that same clean space the exposed films will be unloaded in order to develop them.

Second comes the actual processing of the films in tanks or in dishes (Chapter 15), the fixing and washing of the films. If running water is not available in the darkroom, then films will have to be taken out after fixing to where the water is or where the washing can most conveniently be completed.

F

Here is the reason for forethought about risks to the dry end with the continual passage of wet material.

Thirdly, when the negatives are dry there is the rough check-print to be made. Since bromide paper is to be used, requiring artificial light, there will have to be electric light provided either from an existing lighting circuit or from battery lamps. The development, like the loading and un-loading of films, is best carried out in total darkness, but, for printing, some form of electricity is essential. The minimum equipment is an orange safe-light by which to develop the prints and a light for exposing bromide paper. Methods of working with bromide paper are described in Chapter 16, so need not be considered here.

Finally, I must repeat that the following three factors are all vital: utmost cleanliness, the use of an orderly system, and a rigid division of the darkroom into two parts, a *wet* part and a *dry* part!

15

PROCESSING OF NEGATIVES

In the preceding chapter mention was made of tanks and dishes for processing. The method adopted by the photographer depends upon the amount of work that is to be carried out. Over a complete season, allowing, say, for plans, general views, sections, pottery and small finds, the output may be anything from one hundred to five hundred negatives and, in the case of such large quantities, the *tank* method will be found the best and most economical. The manufacturers of films and plates also supply developers suited to the particular kinds of material, for use with a tank.

The method adopted is to make up a tank of developer (say, 3 gallons) and to use it, until, by use and evaporation, the level sinks to a given mark. After this point is reached it is foolish to continue developing, since the films will not be covered with solution. A replenisher may then be added, bringing the tank up to a safety level. The replenishing is repeated as required until the replenisher is exhausted and the level has once more sunk to the safety limit. The old developer is then thrown away and a fresh tankful made up.

The plates or films are suspended on frames in the solution and the development continues for a length of time governed by the temperature of the developer. This is an extremely cheap and clean method of working, and one which will avoid any dust-spots on the finished negatives, but it is only suitable where large quantities of work are being put through.

On the other hand, if quantities are only small, the dish method is to be preferred. For each batch of negatives to be developed, a fresh solution must then be prepared. I always prefer the tank unless some considerable experience of local conditions has been gained. Dish development, particularly in hot climates, may result in patchy, uneven negatives, especially in inexperienced hands. Whenever dish development is to be used, I recommend soaking the negative first in Tropical Hardener. This ensures that the emulsion, having been soaked for a few minutes, is saturated, and when immersed in the developer will be evenly covered. It is well known that it is essential to rock the dish during development – it is not sufficient to immerse films and let them stand. A gentle 'out of phase' motion is required, not so violent as to slop developer over the bench. Another hint in dish development is to use a dish or tray a size larger than the film, e.g. if the film is $6\frac{1}{2}$ in. $\times$ $8\frac{1}{2}$ in., then a 10 in. $\times$ 8 in. dish should be employed with a generous quantity of developer. Never stint the quantities when developing in a dish. This is one of the main causes of an uneven flow of developer. It is useless to try to develop too many films in the same batch of developer. It only becomes exhausted and the results fall off in quality.

Every emulsion gives the best results in the developer designed for it. Manufacturers list these in all sizes of packing from little 20-oz. tins to 5-gallon tins. Once having chosen the material, therefore, select a developer from among those recommended for it. Formulae for these are always given, but the days are over when the photographer made up his own developers, weighing out the proper quantities of pure chemicals. All kinds of developers are supplied ready mixed in packets to suit all types and quantities of work. At one time the packet developer was a new thing, used mainly by the amateur, but today I doubt if anyone still risks the possibility of weighing errors, when a correctly balanced developer can be obtained simply by dissolving the contents of a packet in hot water.

To digress for a moment from developers to the question of hot water: the experience of my last two seasons have decided me to carry a cheap methylated spirit stove, and a kettle of my own, thus becoming independent of the vagaries of a Primus or of improvising by holding a jug over a flaring piece of cotton wool saturated with methylated. One must have hot water for the developer but these are not the best ways of obtaining it!

Before saying anything more about tanks, let me give another hint on dish development. I have suggested the use of a larger dish than is necessary but I also have at hand an even larger dish which can be used as a lid for both the developer and the hypo. If the photographer is called out or interrupted in any way while a negative is in the dish the lid can be placed over the work for a minute or so. If the darkroom is suddenly invaded (an event not as uncommon as it might be) the lid can be quickly clamped down. It is useful to do this also whenever one wishes to consult the darkroom clock to see how long development has been in progress.

Developers in this country work best at 65° F. In the summer the temperature of the average darkroom is close to this, within a degree or so. Thus, dish development takes generally about six minutes whilst tank development, at the same temperature, may well take double the time. In the tank, of course, there should be at least six or eight films or plates developing at once.

Tanks are generally sold in sets of three: a developing tank

fitted with a floating lid to keep out dust and reduce evaporation, with a cover to fit over it; another for fixing in hypo,
also with a cover; and a washing tank. The films are suspended on hangers, and if plates are being used special
hanging carriers are available. A film, or plate, thus suspended in a tank, is instantly immersed and any dust on the
emulsion is wetted and sinks to the bottom of the tank. It is
my firm belief that this is the method of choice for development on a full-time excavation, where the photographer is
constantly busy.

DEVELOPMENT. The temperature of the developer is taken,
the chart consulted and the time of development set on the
alarm or darkroom clock. On immersion, the clock is started
and the cover placed over the tank to exclude the light. On
completion of developing time, the films are taken from the
developer tank and placed in the hypo tank. I do not think
that an intermediate rinse is essential and, in fact, in the
average field darkroom there is rarely enough room for
another tank even if it were needed. When the solutions for
the developer tanks are made up, the hypo tank is filled at the
same time. When the developer is exhausted, the hypo is discarded with it. Both tanks should then be refilled with fresh
solutions.

WASHING. Once the developing technique has been mas-
tered, the films must be washed. If running water is available
the matter is simple, but if there is no running water, or
water is short, I only wash the negatives sufficiently in the
field to take them back safely to the permanent H.Q. and
re-wash them there.

The system I adopt when water is short is to fill the tank
and place the film in it for a five-minute soak. Then I

slowly pour more water from a bucket into the tank from the height of a foot or two to ensure mixing. This is left to stand for five minutes, when more is added. From time to time half the water in the washing-tank is discarded and replaced with fresh. So far, I have found this to answer quite satisfactorily.

DRYING. Drying the films is a matter for special care. It is best to select a place where there is a draught and no traffic. If people are walking past negatives hung up to dry, they will surely touch them and look at them, no matter how often they are warned not to do so. The non-photographer never realizes how delicate a half-dried emulsion can be, so always find a drying-place which curiosity cannot invade. Drying should be natural, i.e. there is no necessity to soak negatives in methylated spirit unless a print is urgently needed; in that case I always re-wash and dry again. Since the films are clipped on hangers, all that is required is a line of string or wire on which to hang the wire frames, well apart so that they can be reached easily and will not scratch or mark each other.

There is one other aid which may be of use in the field where developing and drying conditions may be difficult. This is 'Teepol', a wetting agent. The solution may be added to developer, hypo or washing water, or can be used as a separate bath. Films and plates immersed in the solution are perfectly wetted all over and so dry without streaks or 'tears'. The material is cheap and would be a boon where the photographer has no long experience in processing.

Tank development of negatives represents to my mind the most reliable method of processing and the most economical, especially if there is going to be a long season or many seasons of work at a definite, settled H.Q. It seems a pity that a set of small tanks is not made commercially to hold one gallon of developer and one of hypo. I did once have a set of tanks made of teak in which I could develop three whole-plates at a time, and they were most satisfactory for the first season. After being stored for a year, they developed cracks and began to leak. These cracks I filled with 'Bostik' but after the second year's storage they opened again. Though these tanks lasted for three seasons' work and paid for themselves, I still think that there is a demand for a set of permanent stainless steel tanks to hold just a gallon of developer. The 3-gallon tanks are cumbersome to transport. Smaller steel tanks, say 12 in. × 4 in. wide, would serve and, in the tropics, might be more easily cooled. Perhaps the larger pottery concerns would make such tanks of thick glazed pottery to the dimensions given. They would be heavy for transportation but ideal in use. The cost might be heavy – I have never enquired, because other things have always had to come first. Speaking of costs, it is perfectly shocking how, when estimates are being worked out for excavation necessities, a scream of horror is heard the moment the photographer's estimate is produced! The attitude of directors is a little more favourable today than it was, but only a little. It must still be improved.

16

PRINT MAKING

In an earlier chapter (Chapter 14, p. 80) it was emphasized that the darkroom should be divided into two parts, a wet side and a dry side. This was because all the work of processing on a site has to be carried out in one room. This is unlike the situation at permanent H.Q., where negatives are developed in one room, dried in another, printed in a third. Living or working in one room is not difficult, but it must be orderly. Every operation should be finished before the next begins, so that it is advisable to have a place for everything to which it is returned after use.

Let us assume, then, that we have produced negatives and now have to make prints of them for the approval of the Director of Excavations.

The dry side will be used for printing because we are handling bromide paper and negatives. The negatives are very valuable, having cost time and labour to produce, so care must be taken to ensure that they do not become spotted with drops of water or solutions. Work on the paper and negatives must therefore be carried out at a safe distance from the place where the prints will be developed.

Now, first, let us consider bromide paper. This printing paper consists of an emulsion spread on a well-made paper base. It must have an exceptionally good base because it has to be immersed in developer and hypo and has to endure prolonged washing in water and then drying. The emulsion on the paper, which is not colour-sensitive, is made in several grades of contrast, both to enable any large differences in contrast in the negative to be corrected and to reproduce faithfully the desirable qualities that the negative already has. As with negative materials, bromide or gaslight ('contact' as the latter is known) is always of an extremely high standard of quality and constancy of speed and gradation. It is obtainable in four or five grades, but for most purposes three grades are all that need be carried in the field – in fact, two should be sufficient for producing rough check-prints and the larger choice of grades left for the making of the finished print.

In the studio or permanent H.Q., or if a reputable firm is employed to make the finished prints, the exposure is made on a printing box. The size of this prohibits its use in the field, so when 'on location' it is usual to expose the paper by means of a printing frame. As with the exposing and processing of the negative material we had two or more constants, so with printing one should establish respective constants for light, the distance of the frame from the light and the temperature of the developer. When working in a confined space the dry end or side should be cleared, the exposing light installed at one end of the bench or table (or it may be hung above it) and the frame placed at least two feet from the light source, farther if practicable. A larger distance between light and paper will mean that exposures will be longer. This is an advantage, because it will then be possible to obtain more contrast by shading the negative in its less dense parts; also, if several prints are to be made, timing errors will be reduced if the exposure lasts for 20 seconds as against perhaps 3 seconds with the light no more than two feet distant. Another advantage is that, if the light source is a fair distance away, one becomes accustomed to judging the amount of exposure required by various types of negatives *at that distance*. Hence there will be less waste of material.

Negatives vary in quality a great deal, as they must – some being taken in strong sun, others in dull light. They are, consequently, seldom of even printing density, and some at least will need to have the shadow detail held back whilst the highlights are printed up. This is made so much easier if there is plenty of time in which to do it, and there will be time enough if the light source is well away from the printing frame.

Negatives taken under all sorts of conditions will entirely differ in their degree of contrast between highlight and shadow, and it is here that the choice of a grade of paper to suit the particular negative comes in. A detail photograph of iron implements on dark earth in a dull light might produce a flat negative without much contrast in highlights or shadows, so the missing contrast must be built up during printing with a contrasting paper. On the other hand, a photograph of a general view, taken in strong sunlight with a cloud effect, may be a little dense, full of contrasts which have to be softened down. A soft grade of paper is then used. Again, a group of light-coloured pots photographed against a black background may, on the negative, be dense in the highlights on the pots. If a contrast paper were used, the print would only show white silhouettes on a black ground. This would be quite useless, for the negative probably had all the surface detail and texture of the pots in it and these were lost by too much contrast. No amount of experiment with exposure on the contrast paper will ever give a good result, so the obvious need is for a soft-grade paper. Adjustments can be made to paper and developer, for the finished print to be used for publication, when everything is to hand. For the rough check-prints, two grades will be sufficient because from these prints the amount of adjustment required by choice of a paper will easily be seen. The potentialities of the negative will then be known sufficiently for it to be passed as satisfactory when work on the particular section portrayed may be resumed.

The darkroom will have to be equipped with a white light for exposing the paper and an orange light for its development. The white exposing light should be controlled by a switch placed in a convenient position. The orange light should be over the wet end, where the print will be developed. The distance of the white light from the frame will be governed by the amount of space at the disposal of the worker. My own method in the field darkroom is to fix the white light, decide at what distance from it I wish to work and mark it. Every time I return to print the standard distance is used. I use a strong printing frame of wood, a sheet of glass to carry my film negative (this is not necessary if plates are used) and a thin pad of folded paper or a sheet of cardboard to ensure perfectly even contact all over between the paper and the negative. The negative and pad are, of course, held in position by the back of the frame, which has stout brass springs sliding under clips when the back is in place.

The procedure is to clean the supporting glass on both sides, place the negative in the frame, emulsion side up, place the paper on the negative, emulsion side down, insert the pad and the back of the frame, place the frame in the set position and expose.

The exposed paper is developed in a dish of a larger size than is absolutely necessary. With developer at 65° F. development takes approximately two minutes. The print is then placed in acid hypo and fixed for ten minutes, washing for another ten minutes. I only make rough prints in the field and the times given are sufficient for these purposes. After washing, each print is blotted with photographic blotting-paper and laid on clean newspaper to dry. The numbering of negatives will be dealt with in the chapter which follows, but I do put a pencil number on the print before closing the frame and usually have a soft black-lead pencil for this job – a hard pencil is liable to mark the negative through the paper.

A warning – avoid copying-ink pencils like the plague. They are used on excavations for other purposes, but bar them from the darkroom. I break and burn them when I find them anywhere near photographic work. The reason is that the dye runs when wet and if one marked print lies on top of the other it stains the emulsion of the print below. If this sort of pencil is even sharpened in the darkroom or workroom the dye-dust can do a great deal of damage by settling on work in progress. This is applicable to any photo-graphic work as well as work in archaeology.

Rough check-prints must be made – there is no other alternative. It is simple enough if a lighting circuit is available or if the site has its own dynamo (even though in the latter case the operation is restricted to hours of work). Where there is no electricity the only thing to do is to use a high-power electric hand lamp of the type used by night-watch-men. These have quite a long life and can be used for ex-posing bromide paper at a set distance. This distance should be fairly great in order to secure an *even* illumination, and if the protecting glass of the lamp can be exchanged for a piece of ground glass, the evenness of lighting will be materially improved. For overseas excavations, where electricity is unlikely to be available, these lamps are ideal. Spare batteries and bulbs are required, but the usual protest at the expense will surely be made when these are listed for purchase!

It is possible, where electric lighting in any form is not available, to expose and develop by daylight through a shutter in the wall of the darkroom. I have used this method in India. The shutter consisted of a sheet of red glass, and developing was done by the light filtered through it. When an exposure was required the printing frame was placed on a shelf in front of the red glass, the shutter drawn away to admit daylight and slid back on completion of the exposure. It all sounds very simple, but with the variation in quality of light during the day and the varying density of negatives, print quality left much to be desired.

The foregoing has dealt mainly with the printing of individually-exposed negatives of a large size, although the procedure is just the same for smaller sizes of the order of 9×12cm. Perhaps something should be said in addition about the use of the miniature or ordinary roll film of the 120 size.

For work in the field, the 35-mm. is excluded as far as I am concerned, even if only the short, 12-frame, length of roll is used. In any case the developing of a roll-film negative must wait until the whole roll is exposed, unless there is to be enormous waste of material. The film should be processed in one of the tanks sold for the purpose and a fine-grain developer should be used because the resulting small negative has to be enlarged to obtain a useful print. Developing and drying present no difficulty, using a little wetting agent to help drying, but the printing is a different matter. A contact print from a small negative is useless, even as a check. There must be a print of reasonable size to examine for correct inclusion of all the details. To obtain a reasonably-sized print from these small negatives, enlargement is necessary. This means that the darkroom will have to be equipped with electricity for the enlarger and this is additional equipment to be transported at some expense. If small-camera work is insisted on and carefully carried out, I see no reason why there should not be quick production of prints. The method, using an enlarger, is about the same as for the individual exposures. However, waste seems inevitable if a print is required in a hurry, for at least part of the unexposed reel would have, on occasion, to be sacrificed for the sake of speed. Darkroom procedure for developing the negatives and the making of prints is almost the same. The two or three grades of paper are still required.

Apart from shading (or 'controlling' as it is now called) the negatives when printing, I do little else with the print in the field. There is seldom time for chemical treatment with ferricyanide and hypo for the reduction of dense portions of negatives or prints – these things are best left until a fully-equipped darkroom is available. With careful exposure, shading and adjusting the light, there should be no need for a great deal of this kind of thing. The same applies to intensification of negatives. If either reduction or intensification is required, the negatives must be thoroughly washed first. Proper field-work should not really need treatment of this kind at all. Only negatives of plans and drawings occasionally need intensification or need 'cutting' to clear any fine hatching work in a drawing. I never attempt to glaze in the field – again, there is rarely time and it is not an essential until prints are wanted for work on the eventual publication.

All solutions for bromide printing are best kept at the wet end of the room. Developer for bromide paper is generally made up in a concentrated form, about 20oz. at a time, and kept when made up in a *brown* glass Winchester bottle. (It keeps better in the dark-brown bottle.) For use, it is customary to take one part concentrated developer and three parts water, or 1 and 1 if extra contrast is required. Like the negative developer, it can be obtained in tins already weighed for use. Once the operator is accustomed to the working of a selected developer, the tone-range of the bromide paper, and the established constants of light, distance of light from the negative and developer-temperature, good-quality prints will be produced in a very short time.

Most of the earlier chapters have dealt with general archaeological photographic requirements, with illustrations mainly from the U.K., because the subjects discussed are applicable to any excavation, anywhere. Special problems such as bringing down solutions to an easy working temperature in hot climates are, however, important in this particular context. Like every piece of work in archaeology, each such problem must be met with the facilities of the particular site and locality in view. No general rule is applicable to all, and space forbids suggesting solutions for every possible contingency.

There is one thing on overseas excavations that must be considered with special care, and that is the water. Water for making up solutions, especially developer, should be as free from impurities as possible. On one site I used the drinking water for my developer. This cost me a considerable decrease in popularity, but it had to be done. Water for hypo, providing it is clean, need cause no worry, and washing water is generally acceptable if it is not too gritty. Here Tropical Hardener is useful – films soaked in it before development need no wiping off with cotton wool when hung up to dry, thus avoiding possible damage from grit to the emulsion.

In one place, on account of windborne dust and sand, I was obliged to bottle developer and hypo, pouring in and out of the tanks each time I developed. In Great Britain the tanks are safe enough with the covers on, but blown sand

12. CHOOSING THE CORRECT POSITION AND LIGHT.
Above: *Roman bath taken at noon to avoid figure shadows on the stonework and to give good relief to the drapery. Yellow filter.* Below: Counterlight shows up well the various stages of rebuilding. A lens of long focal length, well shielded with a piece of cardboard, was used from above without a filter.

13. *WRONG PRINTING PAPER can ruin the best of photographs. These two pictures, prints from the same negative, are extreme illustrations of this. The upper one was printed on a soft-grade paper; for the lower one a harder grade was correctly chosen in order to give greater contrast to the layers.*

penetrates everywhere. Field work in Bengal, in any season, was a nightmare and ice was hard to come by. At one place I sank a pit (in the shade) four feet deep, lined it with thick concrete and had a close-fitting lid put on it. Developer and hypo in bottles kept very well there. At this place, too, it was necessary to filter all the water for solutions before boiling. On other occasions I kept developer in locally-made 'chatties', standing them in a tray full of water and covering them with a piece of thick blanket soaked with water, the whole being placed to catch every draught. At the other extreme, I have sometimes had to heat the developer to a working temperature and short of a greatcoat have had to wear every available garment whilst working in the darkroom.

There cannot be any general rule except to get the developer *down* to as low a temperature as possible in hot places, *up* to 65° where the climate is colder and, if in any doubt, to filter water intended for use with developer. As to cooling, local practice should be followed and the coolest time of day chosen for processing. The temperature of the darkroom should be taken with a thermometer, before actually starting work, to ascertain the coolest time.

G

17

NEGATIVE FILING, RECORDING AND STORAGE

The photographer on the site has yet another task and one
which he alone should do: the recording of the negatives
made. The site notebook has been mentioned, in which the
photographer records details of exposures planned and
actually made. Having made the negatives they must be
marked with the details, and when the rough print has been
made and passed by the Director, the negative, if abroad,
must be stored away in a safe place, or if in the home country
sent back to permanent base by registered post.

To make this keeping of the records complete, the negative, before a rough check-print is made from it, should be
given a serial number. This should include the name of the
excavation and the year if several seasons' work is contem-
plated. The negative must also bear such details as the site-
letter, the lens used and direction of view on the most
distinctive feature in the photograph. These may best be
written with a mapping pen in Indian ink or white ink, on
the rebate – the clear border at the edge of the film that has
not been exposed. I prefer to use white ink on the negative as
it is more easily seen in the darkroom. Some add the negative
number by scratching the gelatine on the rebate. I do not
recommend this at all. It often causes some confusion if the
negative is not returned to its place immediately after printing and the scratches are hard to read even in daylight.

Great care must be taken of the negative. Even when dry it is liable to be scratched, so to prevent this it is kept in a transparent envelope sold for the purpose. Once the negative and its envelope are numbered, to facilitate finding it again its number and relevant details are entered in a negative register. This has a number of columns in which are recorded

135   COOME 53

SITE A   CAUSEWAY & BASTION

LOOKING E.

1130 hours

STRONG SUN

10″ LENS

JONES IN FOREGROUND

BROMIDE PAPER   GRADE 3

the details on the negative and, eventually, the manner in which prints from that negative were used and whether lantern slides were made from it. Ideally, if the amount of work done warrants it, one should make a card index of negatives, cross-indexed (say) by sites, pits, walls, small finds and general views. This may seem to involve a great deal of unnecessary paper work, but it is justified when demands come in, years later, for prints. This I know to my cost because, in my early days in archaeology, I filed negatives simply under excavation-name and year and to this day I suffer from having to look through hundreds of negatives to find one from which someone requires a print.

The negative register is also very useful in preventing loss of negatives. Some publishers like to make their own prints and they are always most careful in handling borrowed negatives, so that to lend them need cause no concern. Loss by mislaying or failure to return them is not unknown, however, and if a negative is borrowed it should never leave the premises until a note in red ink in the register has been made, giving the name of the borrower and the date. No other details need appear, for there will doubtless be correspondence in the files relating to the loan.

COOME 1953

NEG. NO.	SITE	SECTION	REMARKS
135	A	CAUSEWAY & BASTION LOOKING E.	TREES & UNDERGROWTH REMOVED ILLUS. MAG. SEPT. LANTERN SLIDE 1725

The details to be written on the negative and its envelope should be gathered from the Supervisor of the site in question as soon as the Director has passed the rough prints. If the photography is being done in miniature on the 120 size of film I advocate a reel and serial-number, e.g. REEL 10/8, meaning picture number 8 on reel 10. This makes a simple entry for the register and saves time in turning up the negative.

The reels themselves may be stored in cardboard tub-boxes or, better, in little aluminium cans, with the reel number written large and clearly outside. For 35-mm. film there are two good ways of storing the negative. One is to keep it in the complete reel, numbered as above, or it may be cut into lengths of six negatives or frames and kept in a book specially made for the purpose. The 120-size film ($2\frac{1}{4}$in.× $2\frac{1}{2}$in. or $3\frac{1}{2}$in.× $2\frac{1}{2}$in.) can be cut up into individual negatives and these can be stored in stout envelopes. Filed thus, a great deal of information may be written on the envelope. Alternatively one of the little books made up of cellophane envelopes could be used. These are easily procured from any photographic dealer. The sort of recording system used does not matter, as long as there *is* a system and a record is kept of every negative made. Where the rough print has not been passed, a second attempt will be all the easier for the details noted concerning the first. The fact that the first attempt was unsatisfactory will be noted on the negative. The second negative will then be labelled as such and referred back to the first, which should also bear a reference to the more success- ful attempt or be scrapped altogether.

If the negatives are to be collected and taken back to H.Q. personally, care should be taken that they are properly packed and stored while awaiting the conclusion of the 'dig'. I recommend packing them in tens or dozens, wrapped in lead foil in cardboard boxes labelled on the outside with the negative numbers. These should be stored until the return home in a metal box kept in the Excavation office or some other safe place under lock and key, not in the darkroom. There may, perhaps, be negatives made by individual members of the expedition who may hand them over to the excavation. These also should be bagged, numbered, regis- tered and a note made of their origin. Back at home other negatives of site plans, groups of pots, potsherds, groups of cleaned small finds and other material relating to the site may be made. These should also be recorded in the same way and kept with the rest because they form part of the site records, which would not be complete without them.

While we are on the subject of storage, some consideration must be given to the careful storage of the material stocks taken on the expedition. On a large excavation this will represent a considerable sum invested, so that stocks must be properly stored. The material should be kept in a cool dry place. Boxes of film or plates and bromide paper should always be stacked on their edge; never file them flat. They will not be stored for long enough to deteriorate but bromide paper sometimes suffers with stress-marks unless stacked on edge. This will not happen in a single season, but the correct way to keep sensitive material, even when packing to go on the excavation or to leave it, is standing on its edge. When packing never use force to squeeze the boxes in too small a space. They should be packed firmly but not tightly wedged.

Never discard empty material boxes or the metal foil in which the films are wrapped; there is sure to be a use for them at some time during the 'dig'.

Chemicals should also be kept in a dry place. I always have three distinct places on separate shelves if I can – one for negative developer, one for paper developer and at least a separate place for hypo and fixer.

18

FURTHER WORK WITH SITE NEGATIVES

The safe return of the negatives to Base always gives great relief from anxiety. They should be placed in one person's care and during the journey home, whether from overseas or not, should never be out of that person's sight. I make it a rule to keep them and the register in one suitcase and always to carry that myself. The rest of the gear may be left to porters, but the negatives are the most important piece of baggage and no one else handles the bag in which they are.

On return to H.Q. or the permanent home, the negatives are unpacked and checked over to extract those which require re-washing.

The final prints from the negatives are made and handed over to the Director, and from these is made the selection for publication in the eventual excavation report, as well as to illustrate press articles on the subject.

Then follows the photography of small finds which have by now been cleaned and repaired, of mended and restored pottery, and of site plans and drawings for publication. Plans and drawings present no difficulty, but the plates of potsherds and small finds need very careful handling. They are usually photographed with the camera vertical. Plates of small objects are generally arranged in consultation with the Director and the desired grouping then made to conform with the size and format required for the particular journal or 'make-up' of the report. Prints for half-tone blocks must be glossy bromides at least $\frac{1}{4}$ larger than the size of the finished block to allow for reduction by the block-maker. The procedure when laying out such an arrangement of small finds or potsherds is simple. The exact area of the desired block is ruled out in the bottom left-hand corner of a large sheet of white paper. The diagonal of this area is then produced right across the sheet, so that by extending the base, or long side, to enclose whatever area is needed for the display and ruling off the short side at right angles to this base, cutting the diagonal, an area is obtained from which to make the negative in exact proportion to that of the required block. Suitable enlargements or reductions to scale are thus easily made in proportion. The area so marked out on paper is used by placing it under the ground glass. The pieces are arranged, and a scale is placed on the top of the glass within the required area, and the paper is then withdrawn before exposure.

Papers will later be read to various Societies on the subject of the excavation and to illustrate them many lantern slides have to be made. Lantern slides can be really beautiful when projected on a screen up to six or eight feet wide, but their making entails considerable care.

The slides are of emulsion-coated glass $3\frac{1}{4}$ in. $\times$ $3\frac{1}{4}$ in.* They are generally made from the original negatives by reducing through the enlarger, but can also be made by contact as in making a contact print. In both cases, the exposure is made in the normal way and development in a dish follows. It is possible to alter the colour of a slide by shorter or longer

*This is the British standard size. Some American and all Continental slides are $4\frac{1}{4}$ in. $\times$ $3\frac{1}{4}$ in. It seems that the time is now ripe for some international body to secure agreement on an international standard size for slides; I think this will have to happen some day and I believe the size selected will be 2 in. $\times$ 2 in. It may well cause some little trouble at first but will be to everybody's advantage in the end.

development, and a variation of colour from black and white to varying tones of brown helps the eyes of the audience, to say nothing of adding to the beauty of the slide. The plate, so made, is dried and masked to the edges of the picture, and white spots are placed on the face at the top to guide the projectionist. A cover-glass of the same size and thickness is placed over the emulsion side of the slide to protect it from dust, scratches and the heat of the lantern and they are bound together with adhesive paper or plastic tape. Another method of projecting pictures is to use strip film. This method is widely used now, and there is an increasing demand for it, but unless a laboratory is equipped for strip-film work it is better to entrust the work to a firm which makes a speciality of strip film. The best possible glossy prints are supplied to the strip-film makers, numbered on the backs of the prints to give the order in which they are to appear on the screen.

Miniature slides 2 in. × 2 in. can be made in any laboratory. They are a little more difficult to work with on account of their small size, but the procedure is precisely the same as that used for the $3\frac{1}{4}$ in. × $3\frac{1}{4}$ in.

Sometimes an exhibition of the year's or season's work is held and photography plays an important part in such an exhibition. A conference is called of everybody concerned, during which it is decided which and how many photographs will be shown, their size, type of paper and method of mounting. For this purpose enlargements are generally specified, of varying sizes from 12 in. × 15 in. to 40 in. × 30 in. In an exhibition, uniformity of colour and size for the backgrounds is essential. The display boards should be coloured to give the utmost brilliancy to the work; the photographs must not be crowded together but given plenty of room. A larger number of display boards is preferable to too few carrying many pictures huddled together.

19

SOME NOTES
ON COLOUR AND 16MM. CAMERA

Little has been done in the way of colour photography in archaeology, with the exception perhaps of some earth sections and architectural details. At the moment, cost prohibits the making of colour prints, but it is simple to make colour transparencies of the 35-mm. type. Of course, the 35-mm. is not the only negative size available. Colour film in single sheets is available from $2\frac{1}{2}$ in. $\times$ $3\frac{1}{2}$ in. up to $4\frac{3}{4}$ in. $\times$ $6\frac{1}{2}$ in. During one season, I did try the larger size in deep trenches, but the exposure required at the bottom of the trench was too long in comparison with that for the turf line. The rendering of colour was not bad but far from perfect, and in reducing them to lantern slide size, again in colour film, there was too much blue. This may have been due to processing errors.

There are two varieties of colour film – 'daylight' and 'artificial light' – and both are made in 35mm. and the larger sizes. My experience of that one season reconciled me to using 35-mm. size in daylight. Results, using a light-meter, have so far been very good. For general views, pieces of masonry, plaster and so on, in the open and flooded with light (not necessarily strong sun), a relatively short exposure can be used. When the subject is a deep section, the lighting contrast is too much for the material, which has no great latitude, and either the shaded part is under-exposed, or the better-lit upper part over-exposed, with consequent loss in accuracy in the colour-rendering at both extremes. Used within the known limitations, 35-mm. colour shots are quite satisfactory, especially when projected.

To see colour transparencies at their best one must either own or borrow a high-wattage projector. If the hall or room is long and the picture is to be six or eight feet wide the special projector is indispensable. In a small room of 10–12 feet and with a 3-foot frame the small projector gives a bright picture, but if this same projector is tried in a large room, the enlarged image is barely visible. For long projection, 750- or 1,000-watt lamps are needed. I once attended the reading of a paper which was illustrated with 35-mm. colour transparencies. Doubtless, when the slides were 'run through' before the lecture they had been projected in a small room and were sufficiently well lit, but on the occasion of the lecture (a summer afternoon) the same projector was used in a poorly darkened room, to give a picture 6 feet wide with a lamp of only 250 watts. In consequence the slides were a complete failure. For showing colour, the room must be really dark, and the lecturer's reading-lamp should be well shielded from the screen, or even extinguished altogether.

In using colour there are many factors to be considered, all of which must be correctly assessed if the result is to be successful. Some of these are the degree of contrast in the subject, the variation in the colour of the light at different times of day, and the effect of counter-light on exposure time. Misjudgment of any of them can throw the colour-rendering entirely off balance. Mist or haze may distort the colour of the far distance which, despite the use of an ultra-violet or haze filter, will still appear too blue. This does not offend me, for I am content if the colour-rendering of the subject in the foreground is correct, but some critics think otherwise.

Choice of the time of day is important in obtaining the desired atmospheric effect in a colour picture. I have some colour shots of Ludlow Castle taken in the evening light – the mellowness of evening light is there shining on the castle walls. When I went up to it the following morning the colour-impression was of entirely different mood.

In black-and-white photography the quality of the print may be altered by the grade of paper chosen and although the negative emulsion may be exposed according to the light-value at the time there is a certain amount of latitude for later improvement on the negative rendering. This does not exist with colour. It is impossible that the colour film should adjust itself to all the vagaries of light and record it as the photographer would wish to see it. If, as in the early morning or late in the day, the light is red, then the predominant colour will be red, and where it falls on grey stones, for example, will give them a tinge of pink or mauve. Besides, colour affects different observers in different ways. One has only to stand behind the changing groups of people looking at a painting at the Royal Academy and listen to the criticisms – no two are ever alike!

Much progress has already been made in colour photography. I have recently exposed 180 frames and 98 per cent. of them have proved very satisfactory. My only criticism is that the processing of them is sometimes rather poor. This may be due to the large quantities of work during the summer months and rushed processing by the makers. It will be worth while to hold back a proportion and send them for processing at about Christmas time, to see whether there is any difference, purely as an experiment.

I have been most successful with making black-and-white prints from the 35-mm. shots, increasing their size up to 6in.×4in. They are set up before an even light, strong enough to penetrate the dark areas, and the lens shielded closely to eliminate all possibility of reflections or extraneous light. The exposure is made on panchromatic material with a yellow filter.

In the field, where I have been able to photograph an archaeological section in a good light, that is one which is not exposed only in a narrow trench, I feel the results justify the expense of colour. Nevertheless, at the time of writing it seems that we shall not see colour reproductions in most scientific reports in this country for a long time, owing mainly, I suppose, to the high cost of process colour work. Colour was never cheap, that is, good colour work on first-class paper, but when one sees the beautiful colour work displayed by the high-class magazines and their advertising clients, the wish is natural that archaeology could afford more colour, even if in a modest form.

So much for colour in the field, which with the present materials gives excellent results; but colour in the studio with artificial light can become a real problem and I have had a lot of trouble getting results anywhere near the colour of my subjects. Colour in a photographic studio equipped for such a task, with opportunities for immediate processing and constant daily practice, is difficult, therefore the trials of an archaeological photographer, without these advantages, who has to work on colour photography in between quantities of ordinary black-and-white work, are many.

In view of this I set aside a certain time for colour work, during which I try to concentrate entirely on colour.

As I have said in the opening words of this chapter (p. 106) there are two kinds of colour film – daylight and artificial – and if a long series of colour transparencies is to be made the artificial-light type will be the best to use. It is possible to utilize the daylight type for artificial light, by use of the

correct filters: however, there are many factors to be considered when doing this and for the busy man it is better to
use the type of film manufactured for use in artificial light.
Recent work upon coloured wall plaster, coloured models
and colour wash drawings has been successful with the artificial-light film and the correct type of lamp producing the
correct number of heat units. These lamps are available from
the better-known electric lamp manufacturers and they are
made for the particular purpose. I find that the length of
exposure is controlled by the distance of the lamps from the
subject and in each case I expose only by a meter reading.

Plaster fragments I always dampen with water before exposing, in the same manner that I use with the 'biscuit' type
of painted pottery. Plaster that has been treated with Budacryl
will shine if the lamps are too close to the subject; the light
should fall at 45°, but even so treated plaster must be watched
for this sheen.

Then there is the ciné-camera. This is a most interesting
branch of camera work inasmuch as it requires a totally different technique and there is a wide field for this kind of work.
The little I have seen, relating to archaeology, has been just
action pictures on the site mainly of people digging, never of
some vital operation from which so much could be learnt. To
show the actual motions of doing certain jobs in archaeology
might be invaluable for teaching purposes, but the subject
would have to be fully covered and self-explanatory, with a
minimum of talk or titles. It is a simple matter, if sound is
needed, to 'dub' it in when the film is made, but even a series
of still shots would be most useful – and its possibilities have
not yet been scratched. I myself have made several technical
films to show to students, amongst them being 'The Repair
of Pottery' and 'The Treatment of Metals'. In these films the
idea was to illustrate a complete series of operations at once,

so that when students eventually started to work on one of the operations of this nature, they would have some idea of the operations which were to follow. These short films have been most useful, but I found many snags in the making. In conjunction with others I am about to embark upon another, 'Digging Techniques in the Field', and I shall doubtless profit from the snags previously encountered.

The principal requirement is a good working script. It is useless trying to make a film without some form of organization of this nature and it is better not to allow your enthusiasm to run away with you when embarking on a task such as this, nor to try and work without a script. You need the script for a check on your work as it progresses and you will need it more when you come to cut and edit your film. The script is essential whether the work is in the field or in the laboratory or studio; it should contain a brief synopsis of each action that is to take place and specify the amount of film that is to be spent on that action. At least that is the method I adopted with the films I made and it worked very well and was simple. I did not start to use an inch of film until the script had been checked two or three times.

Then I made sure that all the 'props' I might need were to hand and shooting started, each action being photographed after it had been carefully rehearsed and the action timed. This is a boring matter for your 'actors', but is necessary to ensure the correct handling of bottles and measures (if they are used) and I found that a smooth action a little slower than normal (brought about by rehearsal) was most useful.

The lighting of the various subjects which are to be photographed rests mainly upon conditions existing, so I cannot set down any rules except that a film, unlike a still photograph, which is only one frame or picture, will have many hundreds of frames each of which is a photograph and must be properly lit. The light must therefore be with the subject all the time the action takes place, i.e. allowance must be made so that the lighting is even throughout the complete action and not just when action starts.

For instance, if hands are to pick up a bottle and place it on a shelf then the lights must be so arranged that the subject is evenly lit through the sequence of picking up the bottle from the table, lifting it up two feet and placing it upon a shelf. The light must be balanced from table to shelf.

The amount of exposure in each shot will be different, and each will have a differently balanced lighting. A check with the light-meter must therefore be made in the usual way prior to exposing.

The size of the lens aperture must be considered according to whether the shot is a close-up or a medium-length shot and again whether or not the background details are to be in focus (this will be another item specified in the script).

If, in the film, bottles or boxes containing chemicals or other essentials in the operation are to be used, then these should have labels on them, large enough to be easily read when the film is projected. These labels are easily made with a stencilling outfit, the stencilling being done with indian ink on sheets of white paper, and the labels pasted on to the bottles or boxes.

Whilst every effort should be made to make the series of operations filmed obvious (from the labels and the action taken) it will be necessary to have captions or titles to preface each action and sometimes in the middle of an action. My advice is to have these titles made by a reputable trade firm who will give very good value for money in this direction. All that is necessary when the film is finally made is to send the firm a list of the titles and captions needed and, within a few days, back will come your titles correctly photographed and of the correct reading length. Of course, if you have the time there are all sorts of titling devices on the market to enable you to make your own titles, but I honestly think that the trade house does a better job with a considerable saving of your time.

Having shot all you need and preferably a few feet more, of each operation, and having secured the titles, the next and most laborious job is to cut and edit the film. This is done by going back through the script in order to get all the shots and intervening titles in their right order of operations, thereby obtaining a smooth sequence from start to finish. It will probably be necessary to run the result through the projector, and alterations in cutting will have to be made after seeing the result on the screen. Even after the final cutting and finishing, faults in editing will be found and will have to be corrected.

The foregoing, I know, is very brief, and is but the germ of the idea of using 16-mm. or even 8-mm. ciné as a simple and additional method to convey to the student, by photography, the use of the various techniques in archaeology. That it is being done daily in the form of the excellent documentary films produced by the experts in this craft, I know. My aim has been merely to show that it is possible to carry out small specialized pieces of work of this nature with the minimum of facilities, aided by a great deal of ingenuity, inside the laboratory, studio or in the field.

H

PROVISIONING, PACKING AND DISPATCH

The start of an excavation, the first mention of the intention to 'dig X' always kindles another burst of enthusiasm within me. The first whispers that such-and-such a place is proposed for next season sends me flying to the map-cupboard to find out something about it. After all these years I can still hardly contain myself until I am on the train or boat travelling to the 'dig'.

Of course, much organization is required first and the photographic side is only one part, so that there is a great deal to do before putting the loads on the train. First there is the length of the proposed season to be considered, the type of site that is to be excavated, an estimate of the amount of photographic work that will be required, the distance of the nearest town from the dig and its potentialities as a supply-base.

Knowledge of the expected duration of the excavation and of the type of site compared with past excavations enables the photographic requirements to be estimated. Some weeks before the departure date, supplies of film, bromide paper and chemicals are ordered. As a rule, when estimating the amount of material needed, I glance back over the past three or four years' work. If one season consumed more than another, I look for the reason and consider whether anything like it may arise this year. I obtain a Senior Supervisor's opinion of the site, listen to what the Director says about it, and strike an average with some margin for eventualities. Once the number of films to be taken is known the amount of chemicals required follows automatically. Bromide paper is estimated at one sheet per negative plus 25 per cent, with paper envelopes to match.

For example, if 200 sheets of film are required, each needs 1 oz. of developer on the average, so that the estimate will be for ten 20-oz. packets of developer and 250 sheets of bromide paper (150 of contrast grade and 100 of normal grade). This rule-of-thumb method works admirably.

Just before this, camera and lenses have been checked over in spare time and tripods examined for any loose screws. The camera bellows is scrutinized, the camera cleaned and any repairs or adjustments that may be needed are attended to. There is generally a date given on which packages must be ready to be dispatched. Before this, my system is to lay out every single item I am likely to need. Three lists are opened weeks beforehand. Then as fresh additions occur to me they are added to the relevant list. The three list-headings are: Camera and accessories, Darkroom equipment and Stocks. Everything needed under each heading is collected, laid out and ticked off on the list. The camera with its darkslides and lenses is packed first (it usually accompanies me), then the darkroom equipment, safelights, dishes, bottles, measures, jugs, thermometer, tanks, towels, dusters – in fact everything required in setting up a laboratory. These are ticked off the list and placed in special packing-cases with screw-on lids kept for travelling. Then follow stocks of negative material and bromide paper, carefully packed, with sundries such as spare ground-glass screens, brushes and chemicals. These go in another similar packing-case. The chemicals go in first and, although they are in tins, I take care to separate them

from anything else with three layers of newspaper. The miniature camera for colour work and the ciné-camera, if required,
I carry myself, letting personal baggage go with the packing-
cases. Everything must be labelled clearly with large labels,
and the top of each case clearly indicated.

One piece of advice for those going abroad is to have each
case numbered. For each case a contents list is made in
triplicate. Of this, one copy goes to the travel-organizer,
another to the Director of the excavation and one is carried
by the photographer.

Estimating the quantities of materials required is not easy
and mistakes can be disastrous when the site is far from home.
It is advisable to keep a reserve stock at home that can be
forwarded in case of need. Nevertheless, I would sooner have
the materials at hand even if over-estimated, than be in
danger of running short towards the end of an excavation
when things are at their busiest. There was one occasion on
which, before leaving for home, I threw away the very last
of the developer and hypo and had only three spare films left
in the darkslides. Bromide paper and developer were also
finished. So was the excavation, but it was too close a thing
to be comfortable! It is extremely difficult to estimate requirements of 35-mm. colour roll film, so always err on the
lavish side. The stock can always be used up at home provided that it has been carefully stored. It is likely that little
can be purchased near an overseas excavation.

There may be difficulties and annoyances in sending out
materials through the post and clearing them through Cus-
toms. If there is enough notice in advance of the expedition it
often helps to ask the manufacturers to send the goods out
ahead. They will then be properly packed to withstand even
tropical conditions. There may, too, be all sorts of entry permits and other formalities to comply with. If large quantities

are involved the manufacturers sometimes like to deal direct with their agents or stockists overseas. Generally all these points have to be raised and settled at the first conference.

It is best when abroad to carry a spare tripod. One of the folding variety will do, fitted with a detachable tipping head and several spare camera screws. One of these goes into each of the three packing-cases, so that it is unlikely that all will be lost at once.

At home, if the excavation is to have a long season, I find it worth while to reach the site a day or two in advance of the main party. Thus there is time to look round, have the dark-room equipped and be ready to take the first photograph on the word 'go'. It is not always possible but I take pride in being absolutely ready, with the room blacked out, lighting installed and developer and hypo mixed ready to process the first negatives.

Whether on a large or a small excavation, accidents to the camera and equipment may happen. The wind may blow a camera over, a lens can be dropped, filters can be lost or broken in transit. With luck and good management these things should not happen, but it is as well to insure at least the more expensive items of equipment. Replacement value, not first cost, should be considered when insuring. It is a great comfort to be fully insured and it is very easily done. Any reputable agency will send forms by return of post, and the cost should be only about £1 per £100. Then, if anything is lost or destroyed by fire, or in transit, a full reimbursement is obtained without argument. Never under-insure. Prices may rise and a small margin costs little.

This, then, is the end of my story, the composing of which has been my pleasure in many quiet hours. Its purpose is to place in the hands of Site Supervisors and students a simple approach to photography as applied to archaeology. It was never intended to be technically exhaustive or to explain the theory of optics, chemistry or the properties of light. I have particularly avoided the controversy over the merits of the miniature camera versus those of the large field camera. My respect for the worker with the miniature increases as time goes on and as I see more of the results.

The standard of photography coming from small excavations, at least of the work which has passed through my department, is higher than it was before World War II. This is perhaps due in part to the high cost of materials or their scarcity – both factors making for more careful work. At the same time we still see too much indifferent work and the neatness of finish in the subject does on occasion leave something to be desired. There are still heard harrowing stories of professional photographers who have been called in and have charged heavily for work that has proved unsatisfactory, using a hand camera for example when what was needed was a field camera on a stand, but I regard this as a slur on a still rising profession. More probably the cause of failure was that the archaeologist was unable to make clear exactly what was needed to a photographer who could not be expected to have any comprehension of archaeological requirements.

Site Supervisors or students need not be practical photographers (though it is as well to do one's own photography), but they must be able to instruct a photographer as to what is wanted and to see these instructions carried out.

Photography is bound to play a large part in modern archaeology. Most archaeologists are ready to concede this and it is only thoughtlessness and lack of system that produces slipshod work. Through the experience of years of correcting errors in processing, scaling and lack of cleanliness before taking the photograph, there runs as a constant theme the necessity for forethought. Whether the equipment is worth £100 or whether it is a vintage half-plate camera bought 'for a song' at an auction room, it will do what is wanted if sufficient thought is given to the subject's special requirements. Inattention to cleanliness of the subject or to lighting, hasty recording without due consideration for the ultimate purpose of the photograph, will be revealed in the finished printed report or in the lantern slides illustrating a paper.

Photography can be a subject of absorbing interest and my aim has been, both in lectures and in this book, to assist the growth of that interest in others and to create in them a sense of pride in good work. This proper pride added to a lifelong interest will make photography for them what it has been for me – a craft.

INDEX